Mastering the Guitar

A COMPREHENSIVE METHOD FOR TODAY'S GUITARIST!

TECHNIQUE STUDIES

By William Bay &
Mike Christiansen

William Bay

Mike Christiansen

Introduction

Mastering the Guitar is an innovative, exciting, and comprehensive way to learn the guitar. Written in notation and tablature, it covers guitar solo and accompaniment styles ranging from Celtic to Classic to Cajun; from Flamenco to fiddle tunes; from Renaissance to Rock to Reggae; from Baroque to Blues to Bluegrass; and from Latin to Country to Jazz. A special feature of this method is that it teaches both flatpicking and fingerstyle solo and accompaniment techniques.

Mastering the Guitar: Technique Studies is a comprehensive guitar technic book. This in-depth text will give you hundreds of flatpicking <u>and</u> fingerpicking studies, pieces and etudes. Studies are contained in the keys of C, Am, G, Em, D, A, E, F, Dm and Bb. In addition, in each key you will play picking etudes, cross-picking studies, chord studies, contemporary fingerstyle pieces and etudes, and also time-proven classic guitar studies written in notation and tablature! Although this text was written as a technic supplement for the exciting new *Mel Bay Mastering the Guitar Method*, it is so comprehensive and useful that it will serve as an invaluable study guide and daily practice regimen for any guitarist, regardless of the level of ability or methodology!

MEL BAY ®

Basics

Time Signatures

The above examples are the common types of time signatures to be used in this book.

The number of beats per measure.

The type of note receiving one beat.

Beats per measure

A quarter note receives one beat.

Signifies so-called "common time" and is simply another way of designating 4/4 time.

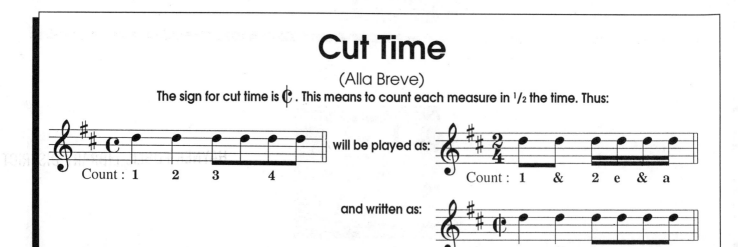

Cut Time
(Alla Breve)
The sign for cut time is ₵. This means to count each measure in 1/2 the time. Thus:

Count : 1   2   3   4

will be played as:

Count : 1   &   2   e   &   a

and written as:

Count : 1   &   2   e   &   a

Table of Notes and Rests

Whole Note	o		Whole Measure Rest	▬
Half Notes	♩ ♩		Half Rest	▬
Quarter Notes	♩ ♩ ♩ ♩		Quarter Rest	𝄽
Eighth Notes	♫ ♫ ♫ ♫		Eighth Rest	𝄾
Sixteenth Notes	♬♬♬♬		Sixteenth Rest	𝄿

Sixteenth Notes

A sixteenth note looks like this: It gets $\frac{1}{4}$ beat, if the bottom number in the time signature is 4.

Several sixteenth notes together look like this: or

A sixteenth rest looks like this:

It takes two sixteenth notes to equal one eighth note, or four sixteenth notes to equal one quarter note.

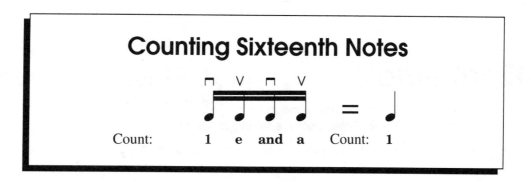

Study

Basics

Triplets

A **triplet** is a group of three notes played in the time of two notes of the same kind.

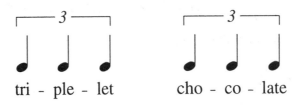

Two-Beat (Quarter Note) Triplets

When three quarter notes have a bracket and a number three under, or above them, this is a quarter note (or a two-beat) triplet.

These three notes are to be played in two beats. The two beats are divided into three equal parts. The two-beat triplet can be counted "tri-pel-et" or it may help to say "cho-co-late."

tri - ple - let   cho - co - late

Usually, the notes in a two-beat triplet are picked down–down–down.

Six-Eight Time

This sign indicates six-eight time.

6 – beats per measure
8 – type of note receiving one beat

An eighth note ♪ = one beat, a quarter note ♩ = two beats, a dotted quarter note ♩. = three beats, and a sixteenth note ♬ = 1/2 beat.

Six-eight time consists of two units containing three beats each.

It will be counted:
1- 2- 3- 4- 5- 6
with the accents on beats one and four.

Learning to Read Tablature

Tablature is a way of writing guitar music which tells you where to find notes. In tablature:

Lines = Strings
Numbers = Frets

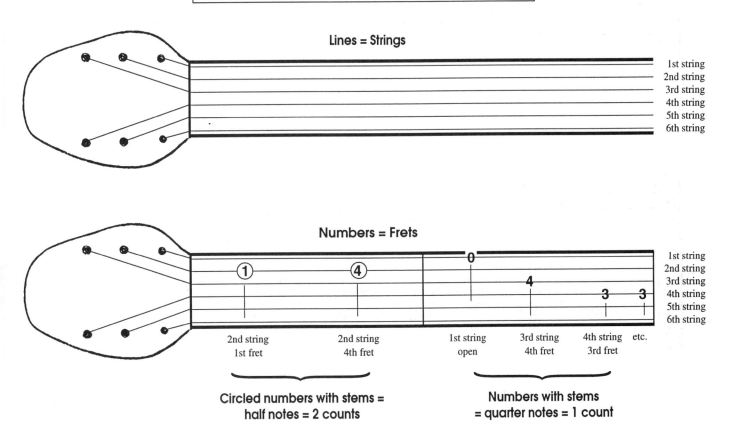

Lines = Strings

1st string
2nd string
3rd string
4th string
5th string
6th string

Numbers = Frets

1st string
2nd string
3rd string
4th string
5th string
6th string

| 2nd string 1st fret | 2nd string 4th fret | 1st string open | 3rd string 4th fret | 4th string 3rd fret | etc. |

Circled numbers with stems = half notes = 2 counts

Numbers with stems = quarter notes = 1 count

Playing Several Notes at Once

When numbers appear right above one another, more than one note is played at the same time.

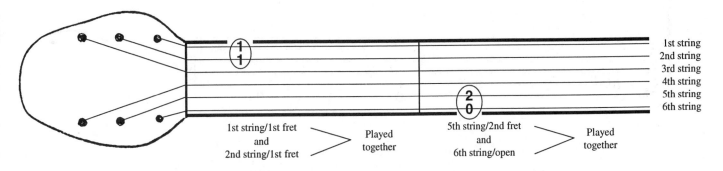

1st string
2nd string
3rd string
4th string
5th string
6th string

1st string/1st fret
and
2nd string/1st fret > Played together

5th string/2nd fret
and
6th string/open > Played together

Circled numbers without stems = whole notes = 4 counts

Basics

Basic Notes

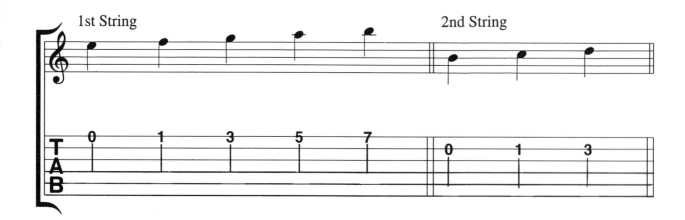

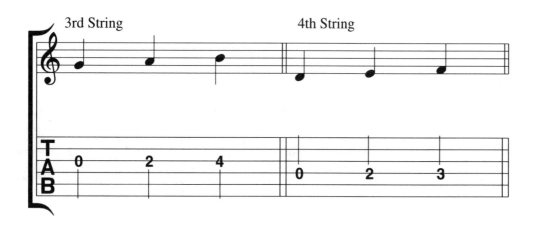

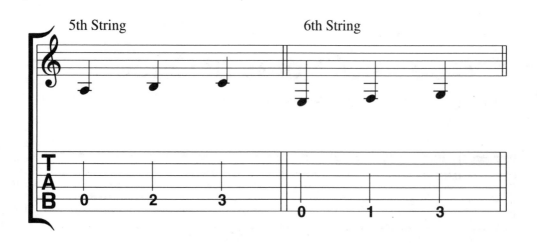

Sharps

A "**sharp**" placed in front of a note *raises* the pitch $1/2$ step or 1 fret. Study the notes below. We will learn more about sharps as we learn specific keys later on.

Basics

1st String

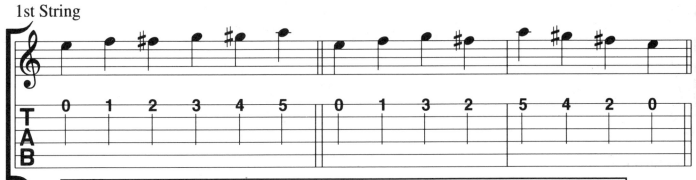

When a note is sharped, all notes of that pitch remain sharped throughout the measure unless a **natural sign (♮)** appears. A natural sign cancels a sharp.

1st String
Sharps & Naturals

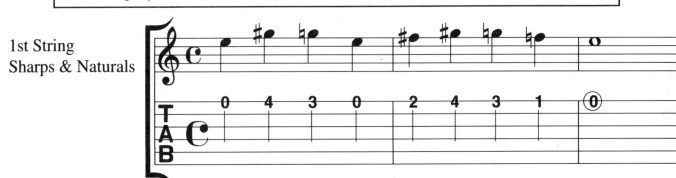

2nd String

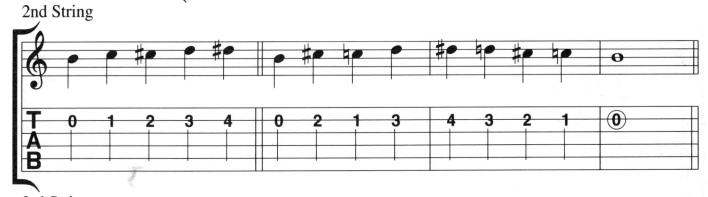

3rd String

4th String

5th String

6th String

Walking Guitar

WB

Flats

A *flat* (♭) placed in front of a note *lowers* the pitch ½ step or one fret. Study the notes below.
A **natural sign** (♮) cancels out a flat.

1st String

2nd String

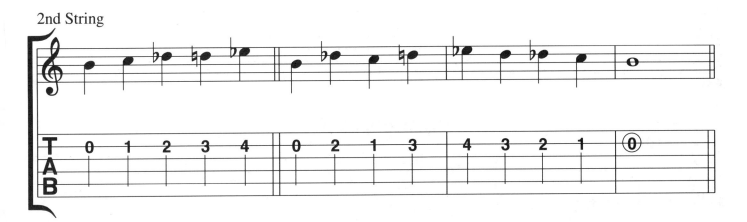

3rd String

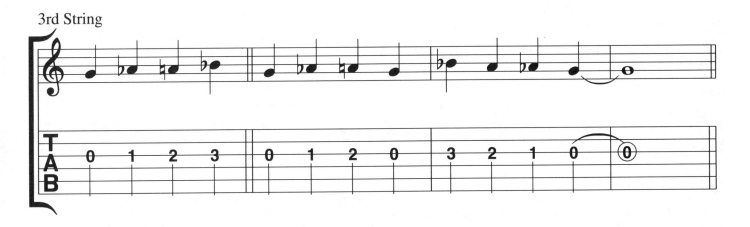

4th String

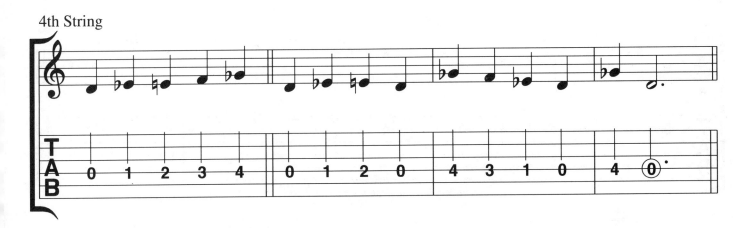

Basics

5th String

6th String

Flatpick Solo
Bright

Benny's Flat

WB

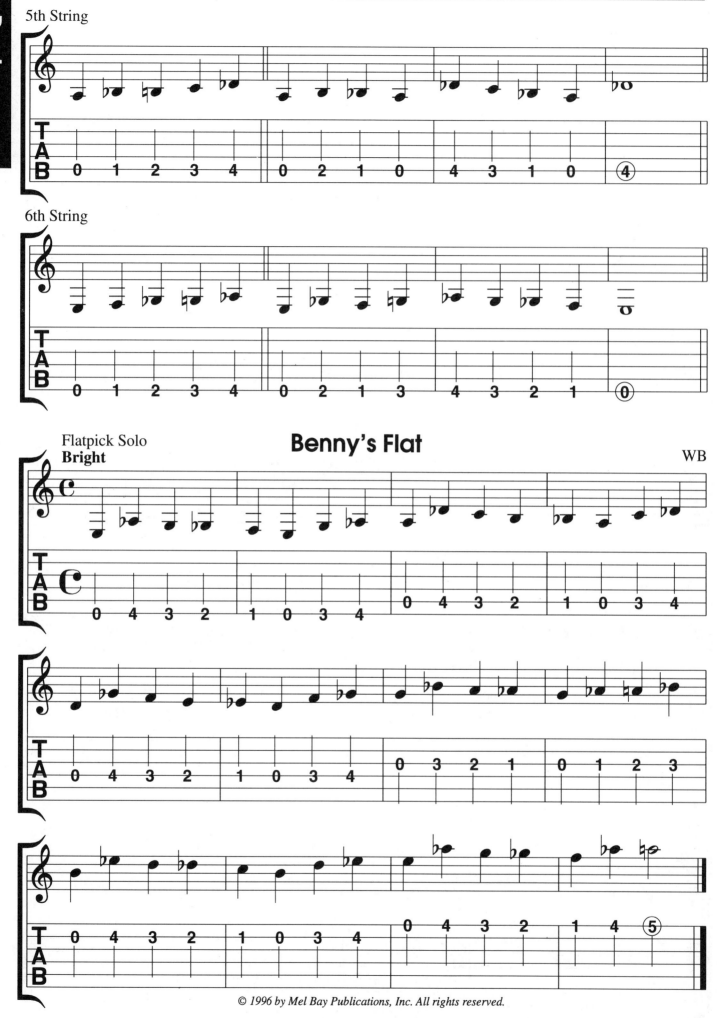

Key of C

Picking Studies

WB

WB

WB

④

⑤

⑥

Key of C

WB

WB

Key of C

WB

Key of C

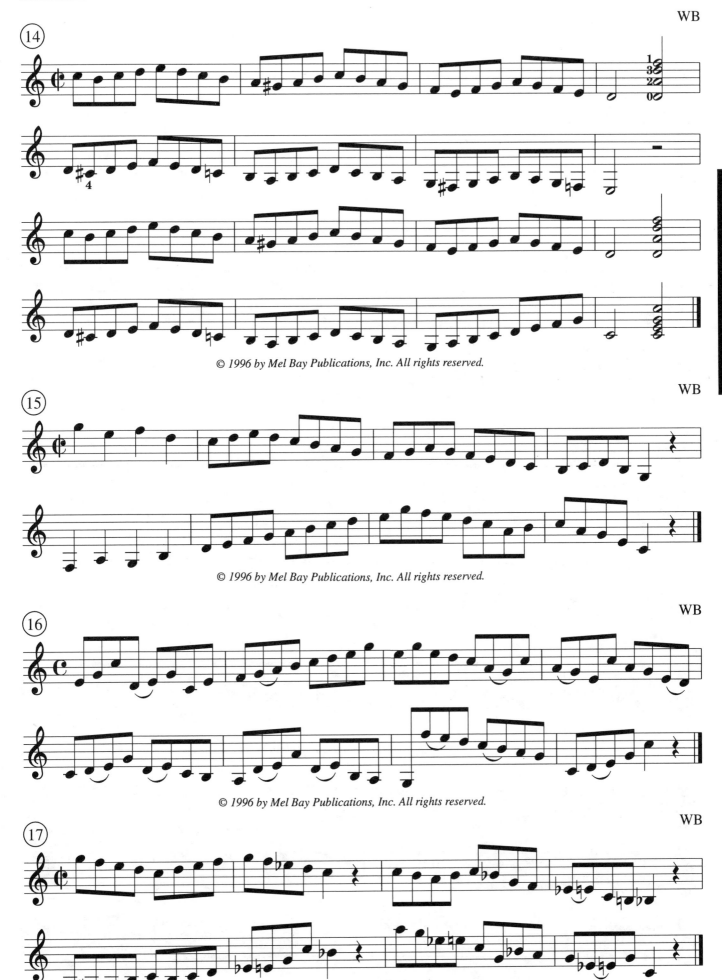

Key of C

Crosspicking Studies

Chord Studies

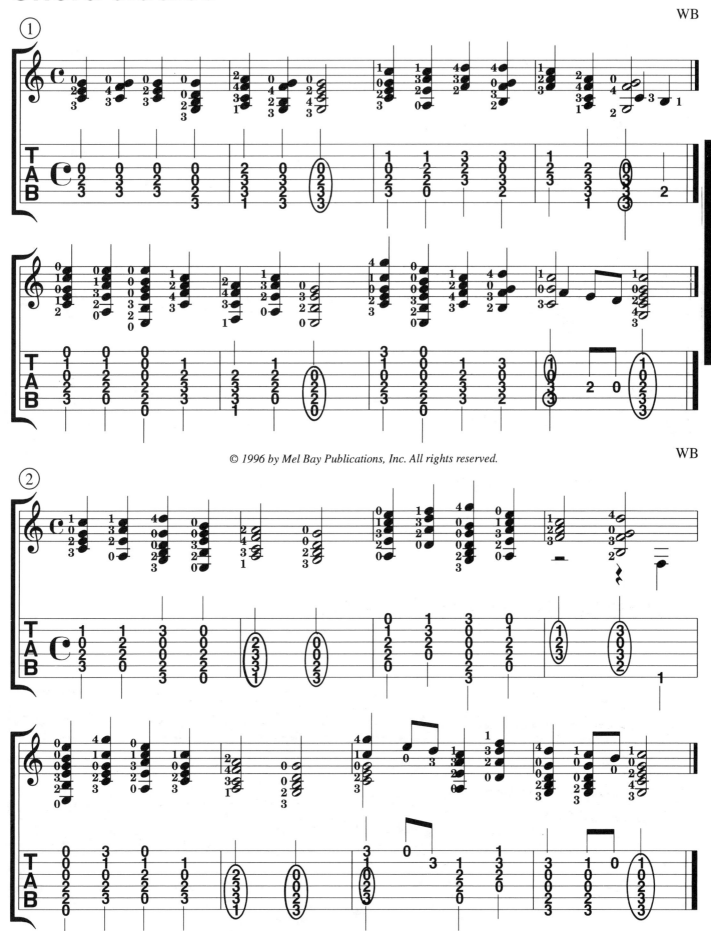

Key of C

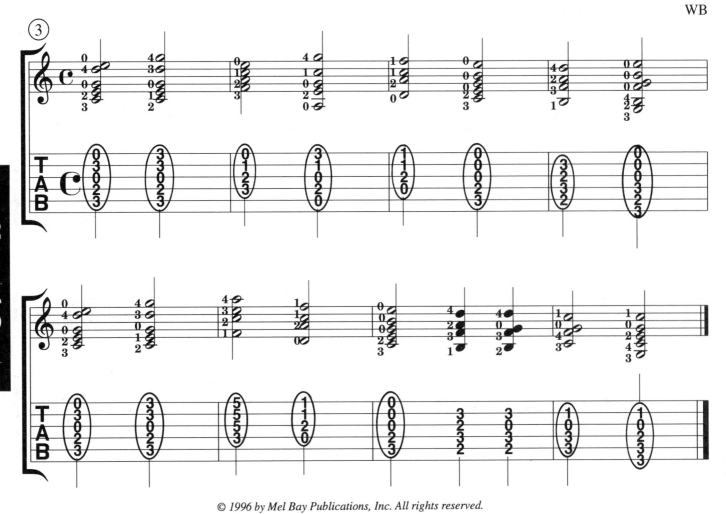

Moveable Finger Patterns

Fingerstyle Studies

First Snow

MC

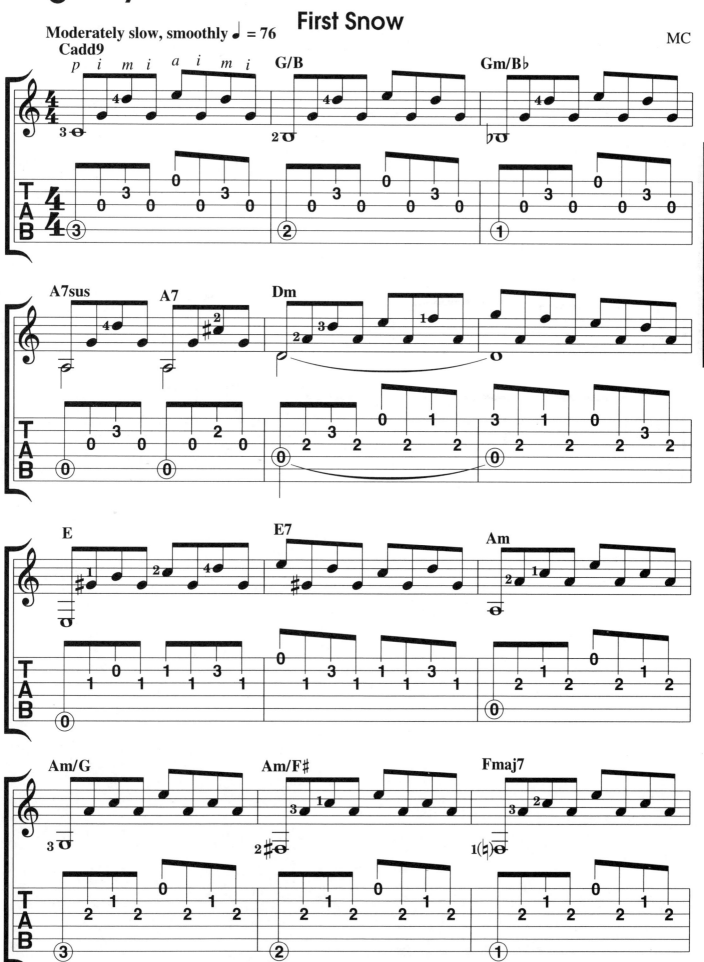

Key of C

Key of C

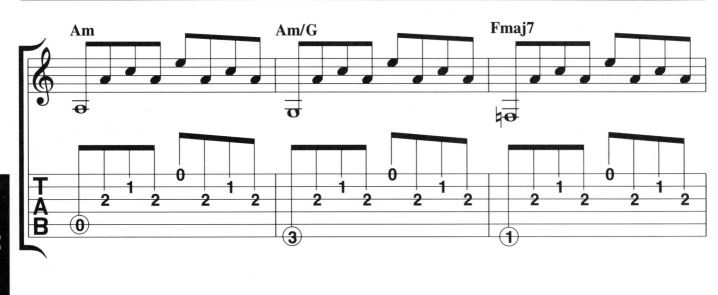

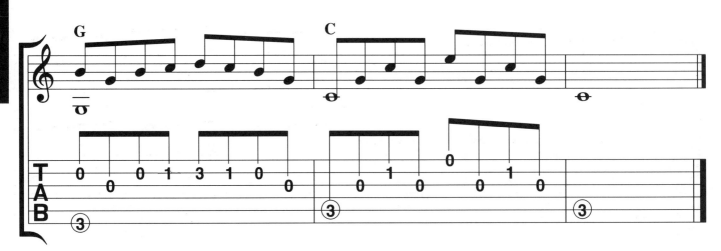

Returning Home

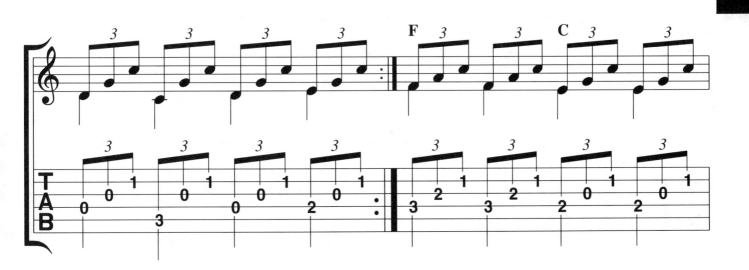

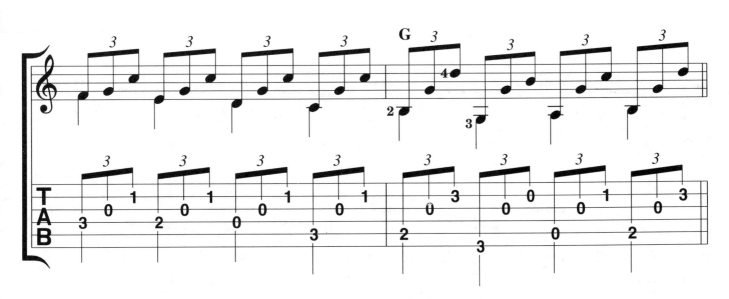

Key of C

Key of C

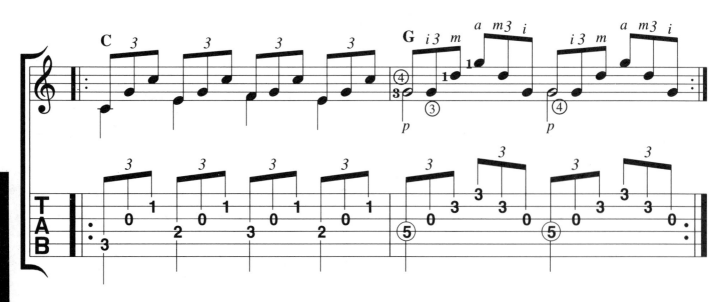

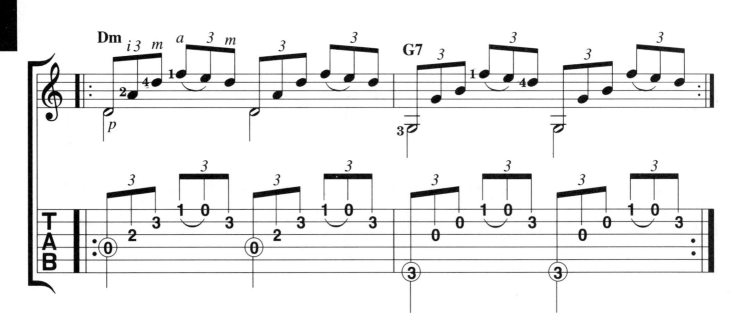

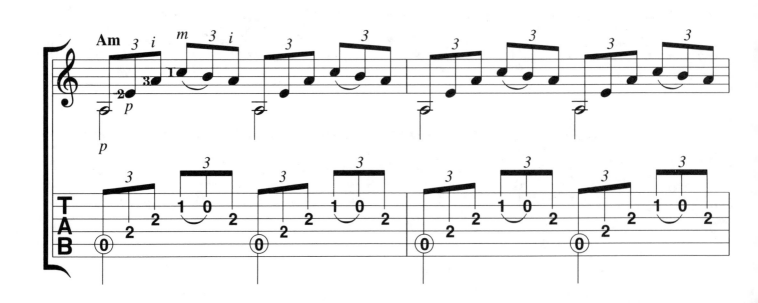

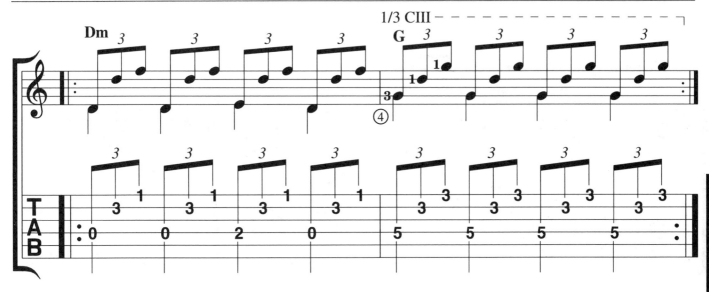

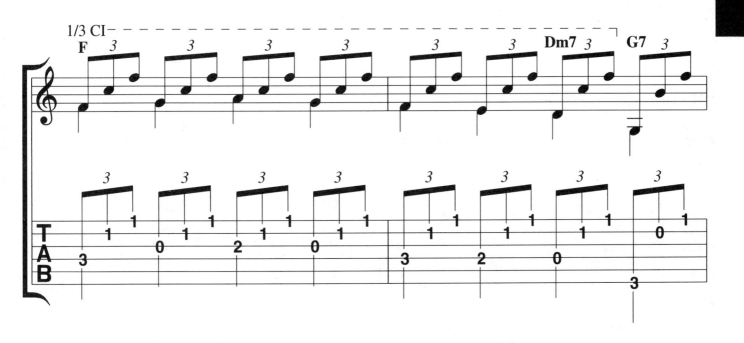

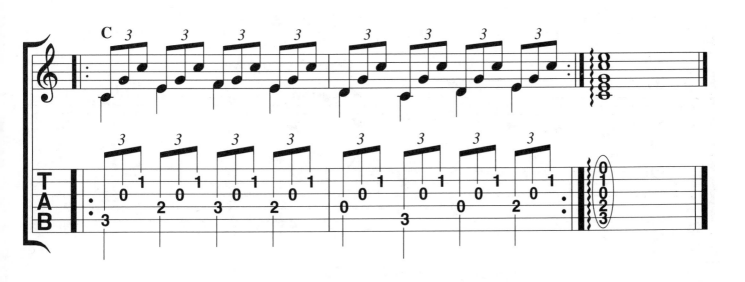

Key of C

Just in Time

MC

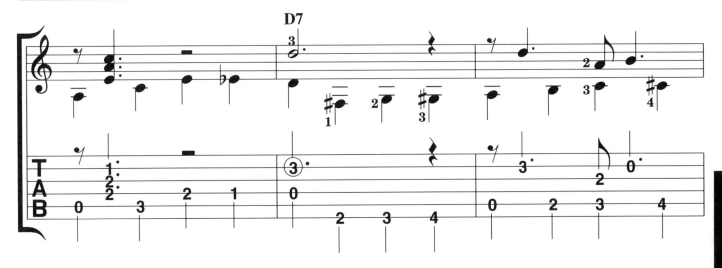

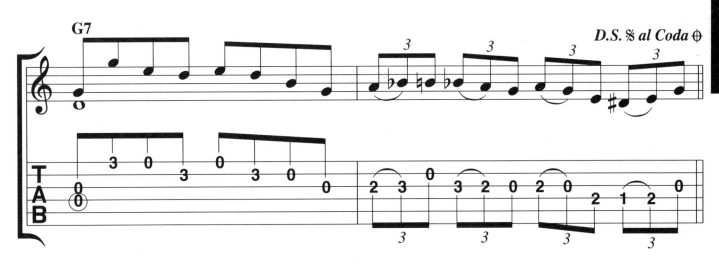

Key of C

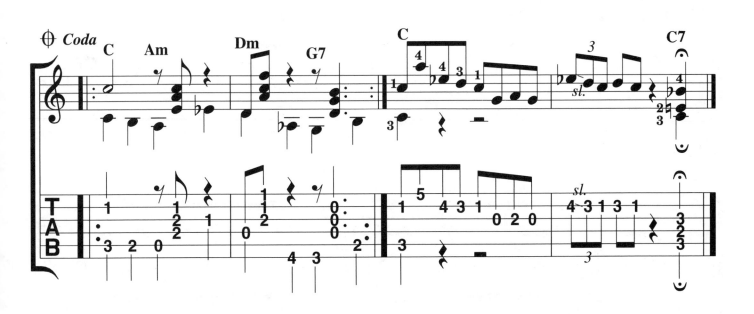

Allegretto

Fernando Sor

Key of C

Key of A minor

Picking Studies

Key of A minor

WB

⑤

WB

⑥

WB

⑦

WB

⑧

Key of A minor

WB

⑨

WB

⑩

WB

⑪

WB

⑫

Key of A minor

Moveable Finger Patterns

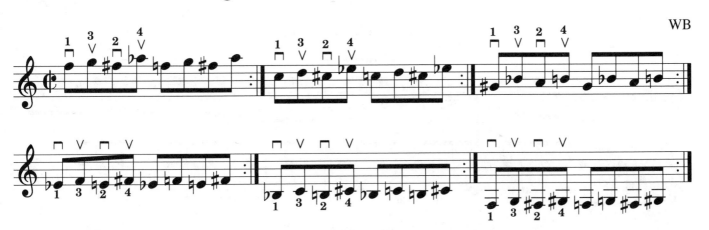

Cross Picking Studies

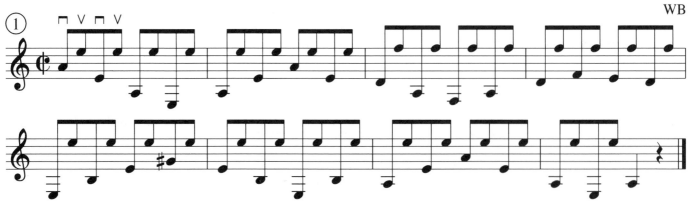

Chord Studies

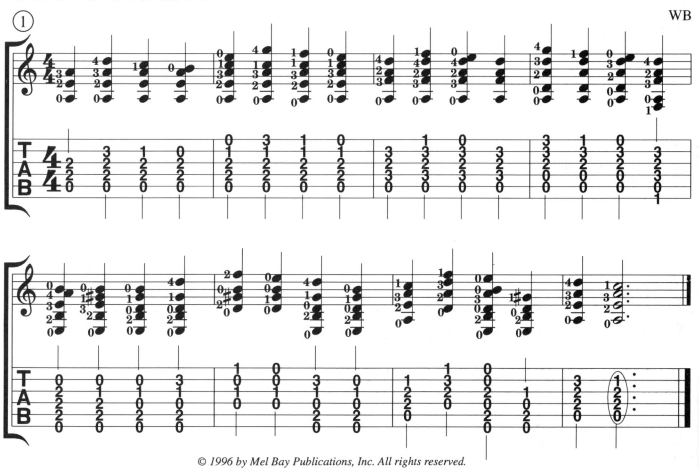

Key of A minor

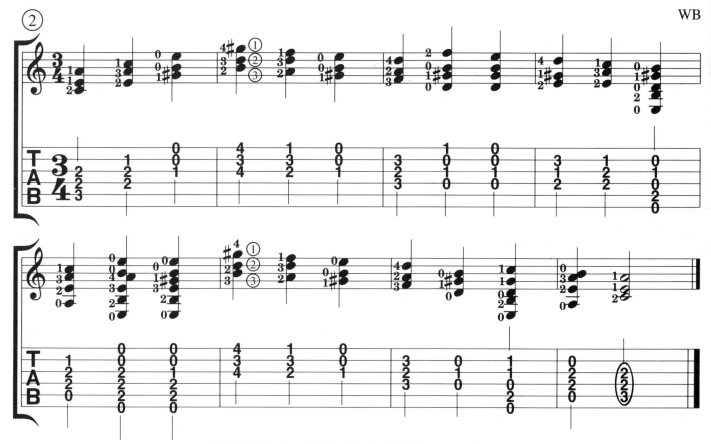

WB

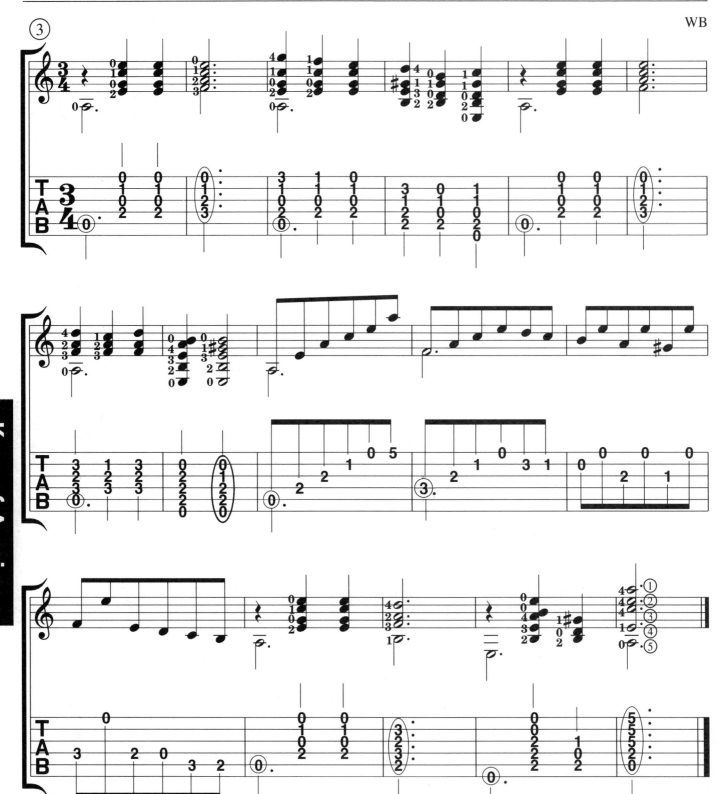

Key of A minor

Fingerstyle Studies

Moderately fast ♩ = 120 (♫ = ♪♪♪)   ## Sneakin' 'Round

Key of A minor

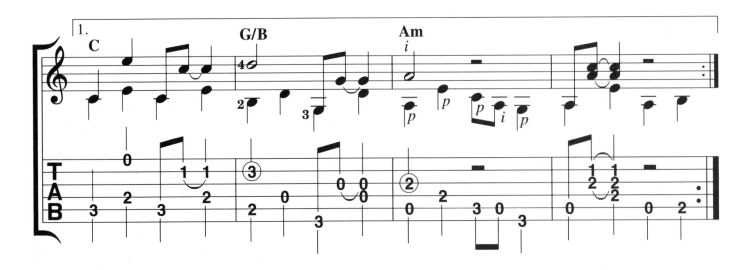

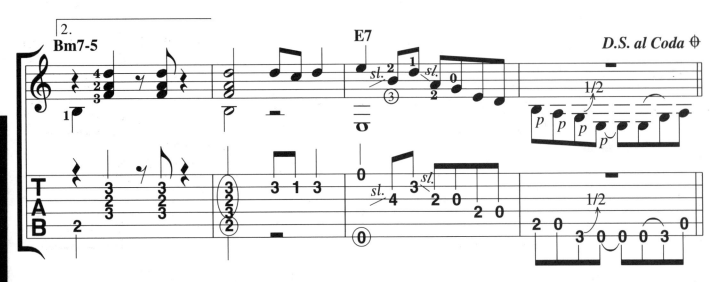

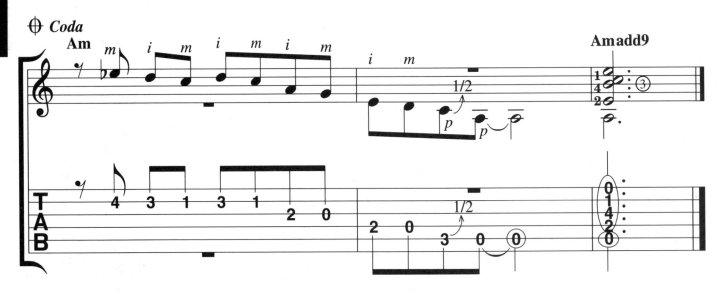

On the Run

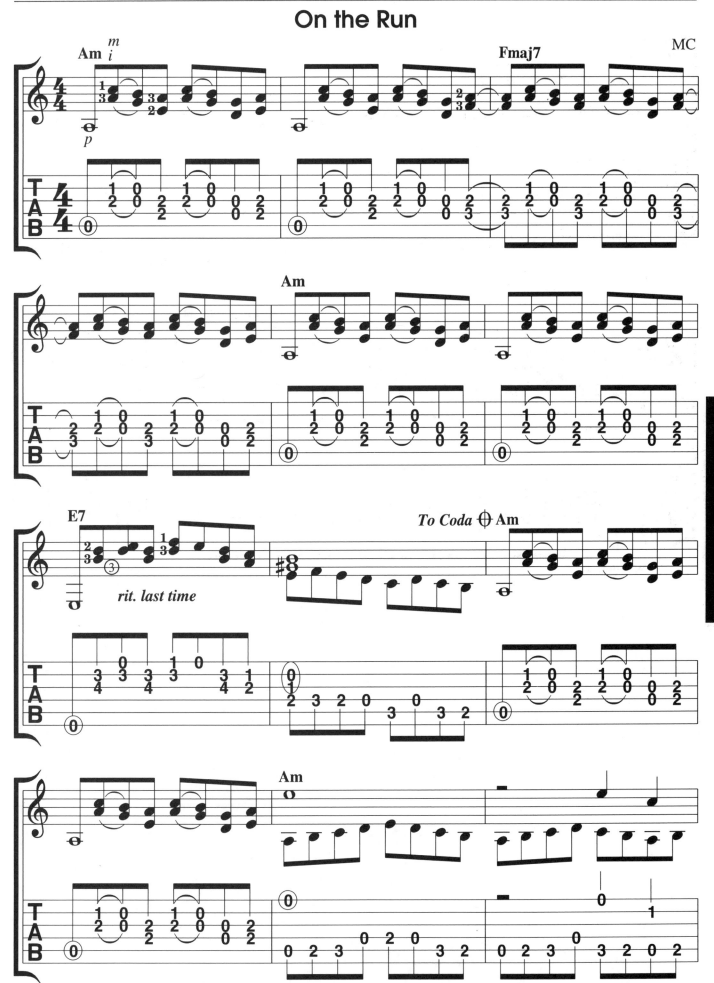

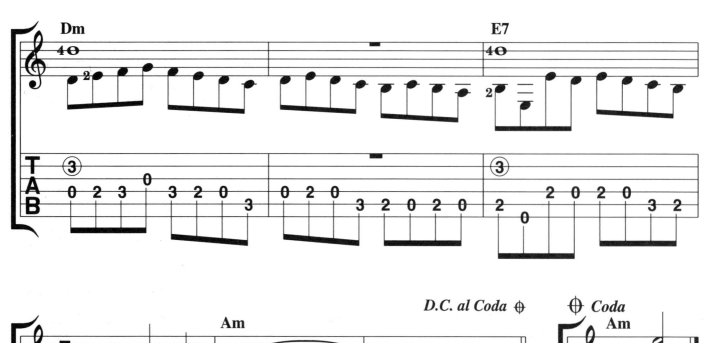

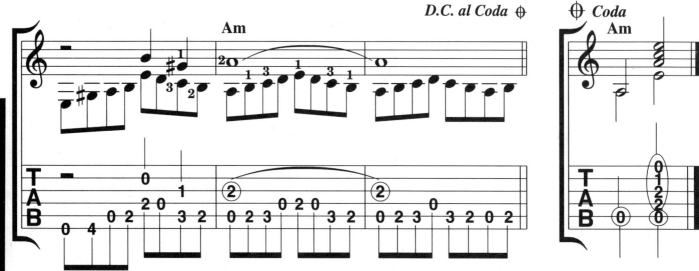

Key of A minor

Andante

Ferdinando Carulli

Key of A minor

Key of A minor

Key of G

Picking Studies

WB

①

WB

②

WB

③

WB

④

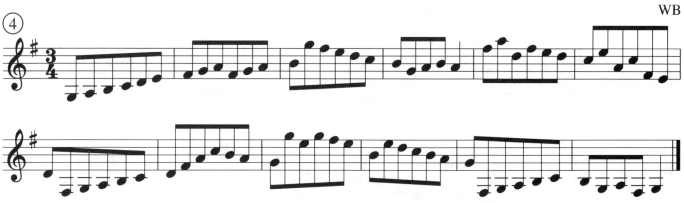

Key of G

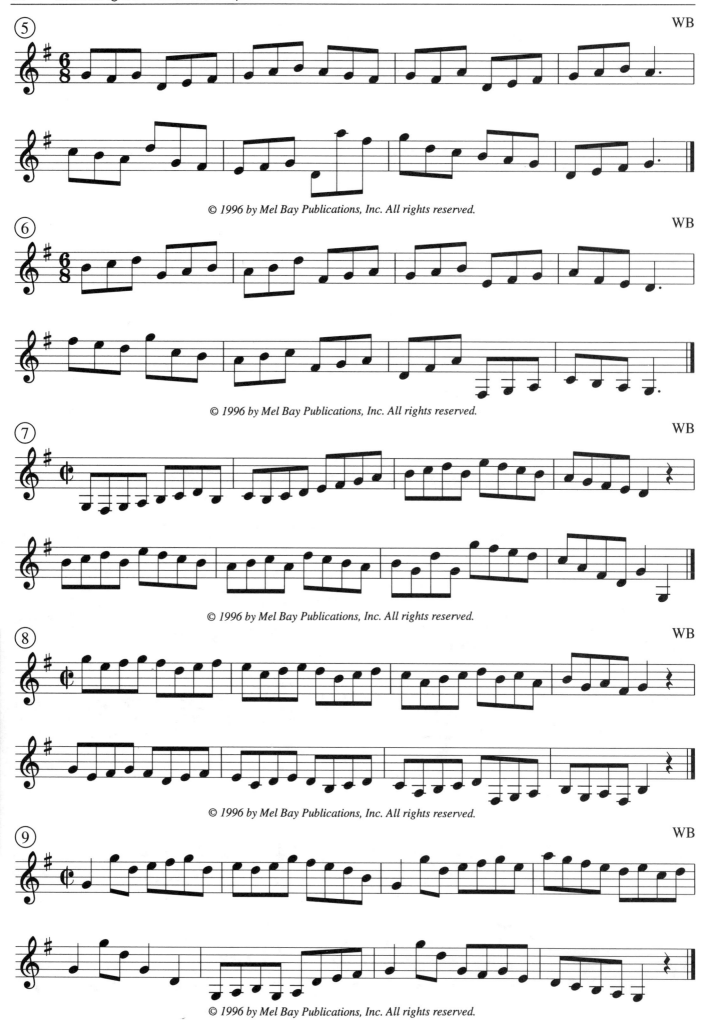

Key of G

Key of G

Cross Picking Studies

WB

WB

WB

WB

Chord Studies

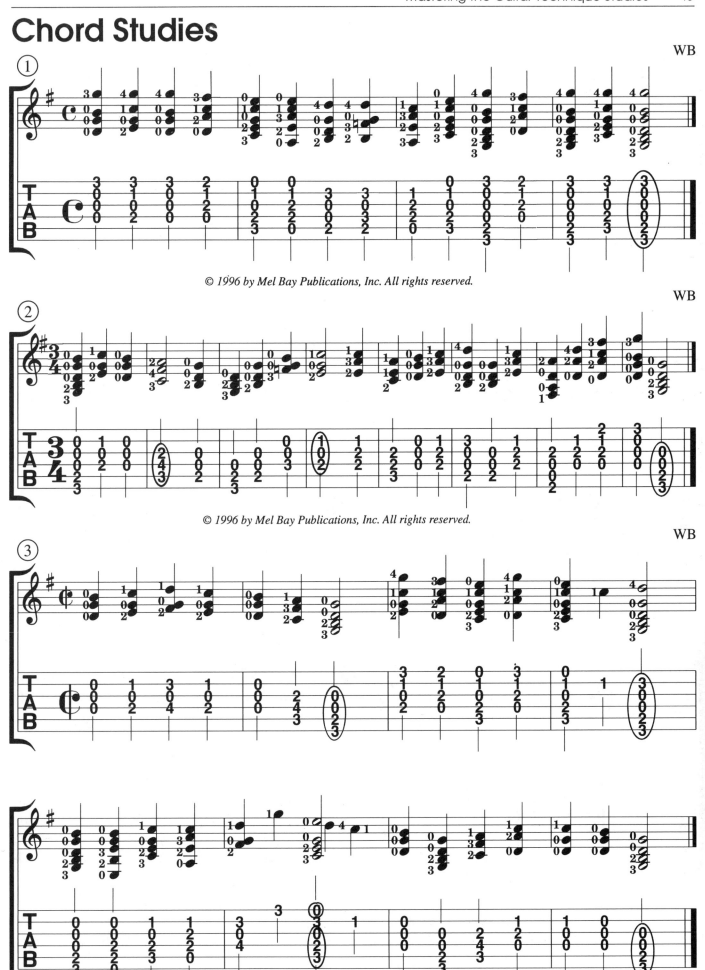

Key of G

WB

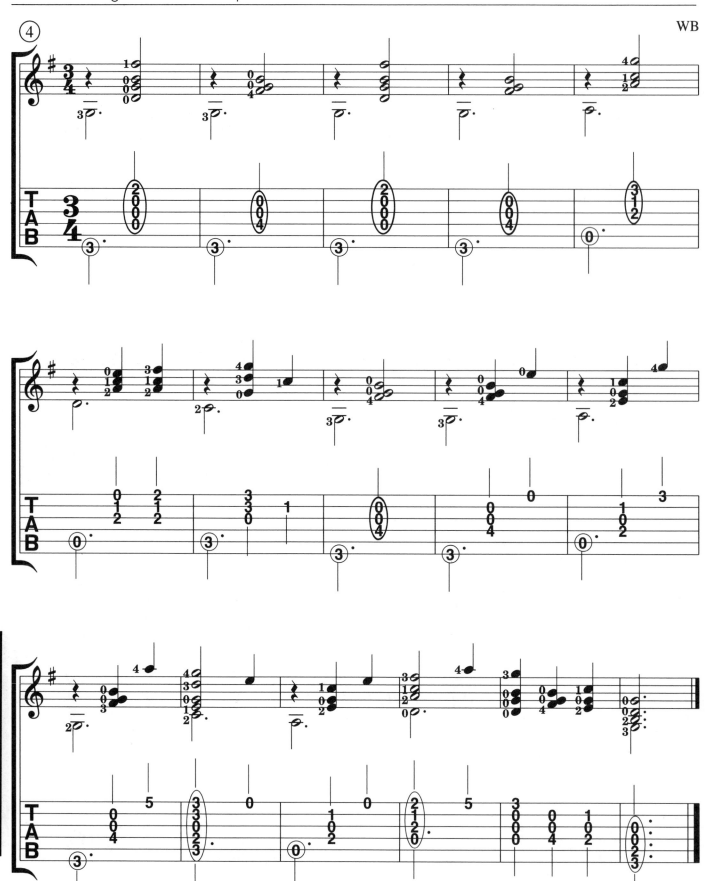

Key of G

Fingerstyle Studies
Reflections of New Hampshire

Key of G

Oscar's Shuffle

MC

Key of G

Key of G

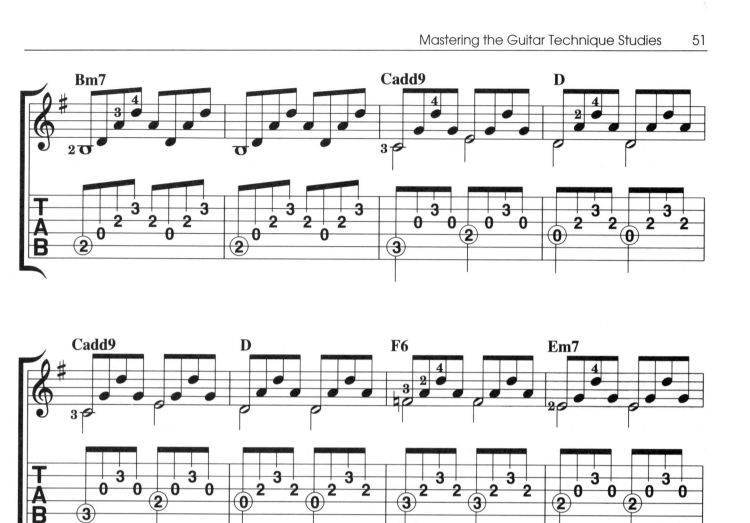

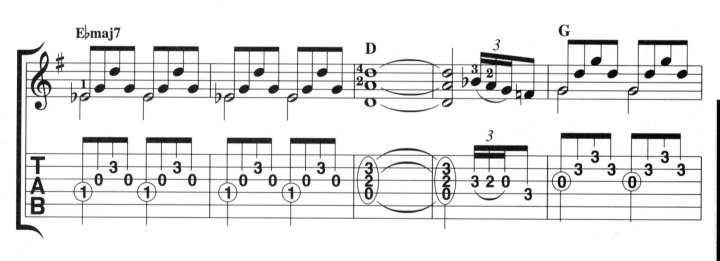

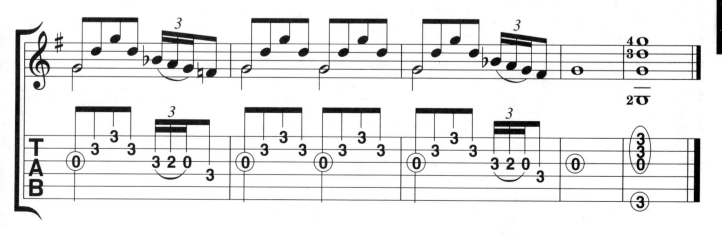

Key of G

Moderato

Ferdinando Carulli

Key of E minor

Picking Studies

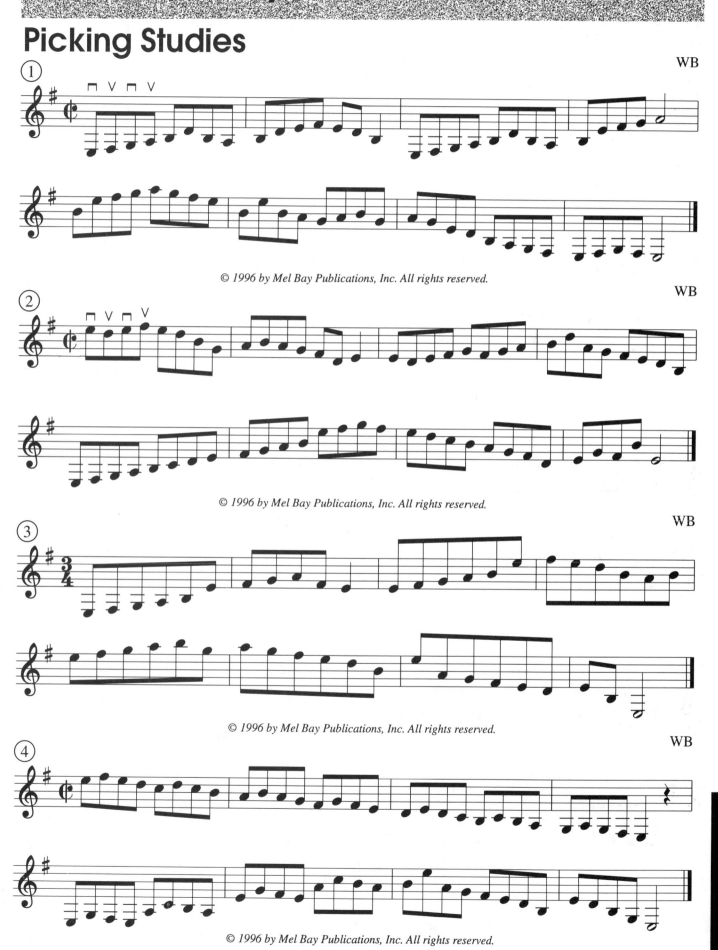

WB

WB

WB

WB

Key of E minor

WB

⑤

WB

⑥

WB

⑦

WB

⑧

Key of E minor

Key of E minor

Cross Picking Studies

Key of E minor

Chord Studies

①

WB

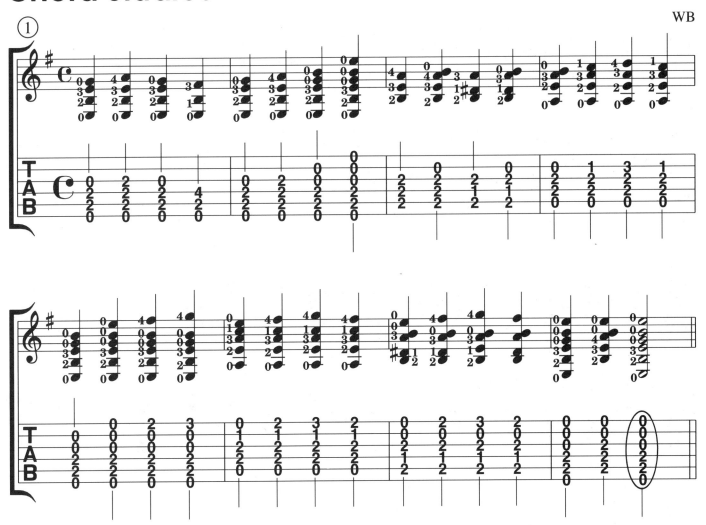

②

WB

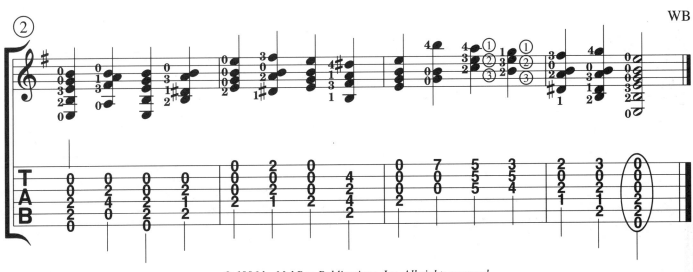

Key of E minor

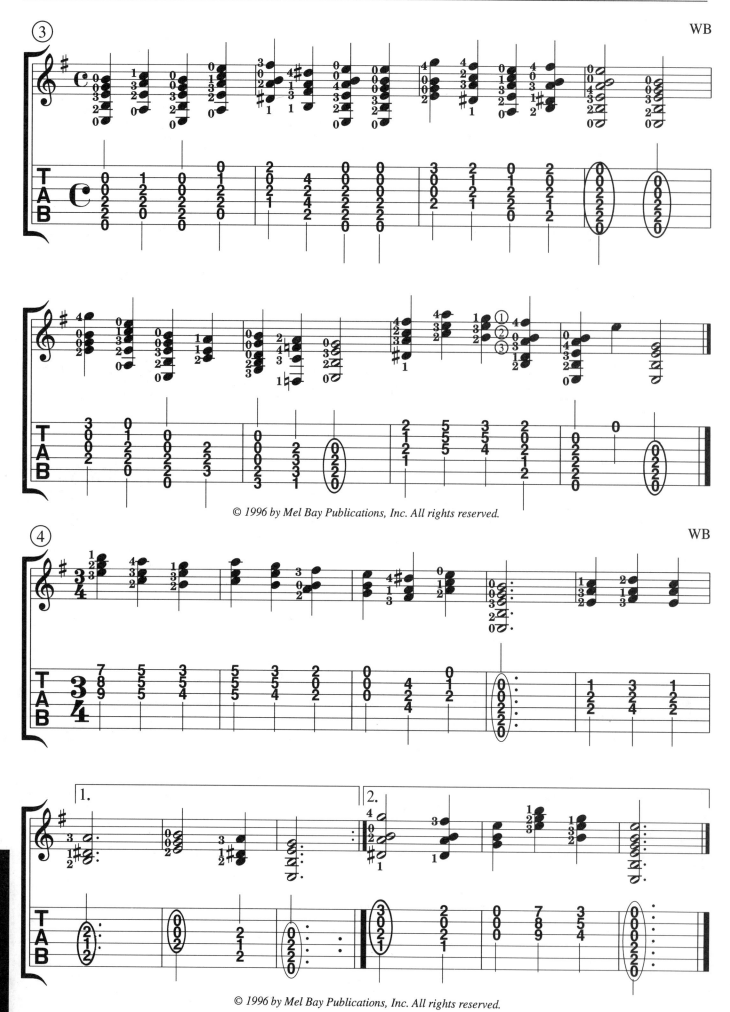

Key of E minor

Fingerstyle Studies

Picasso

MC

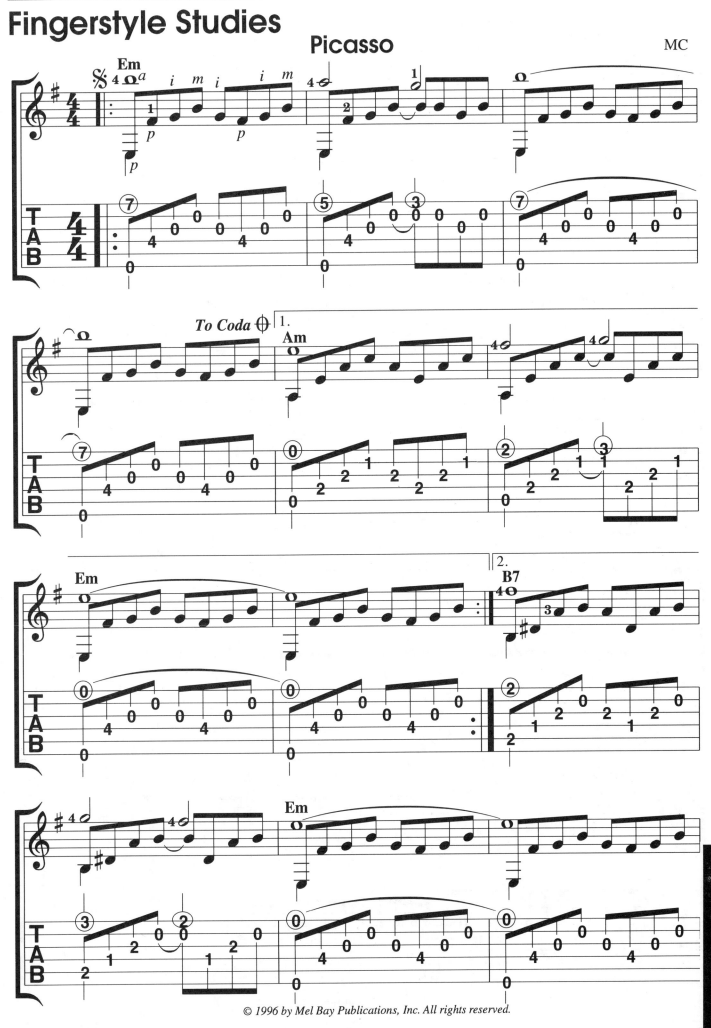

Key of E minor

Key of E minor

The Mysterious Canyon

Smoothly ♩ = 124

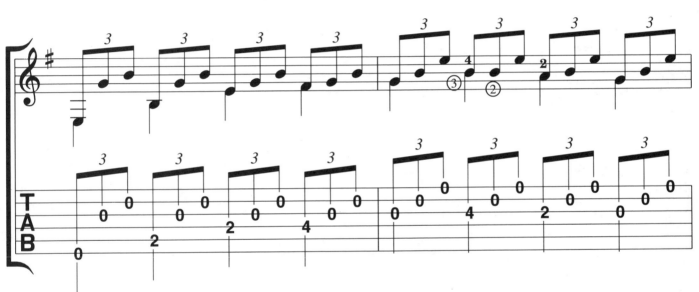

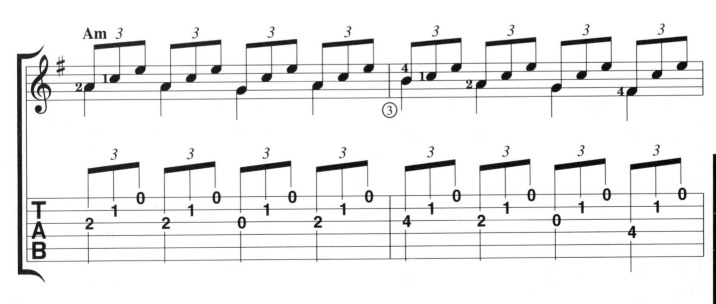

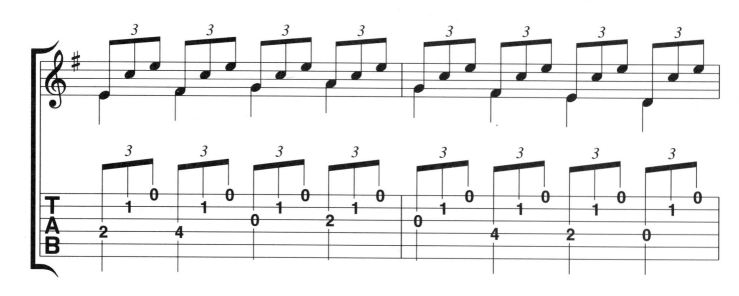

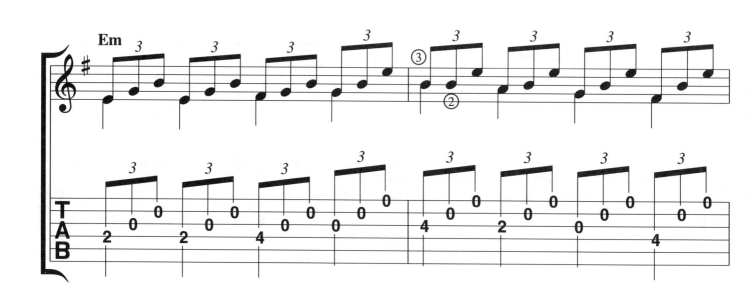

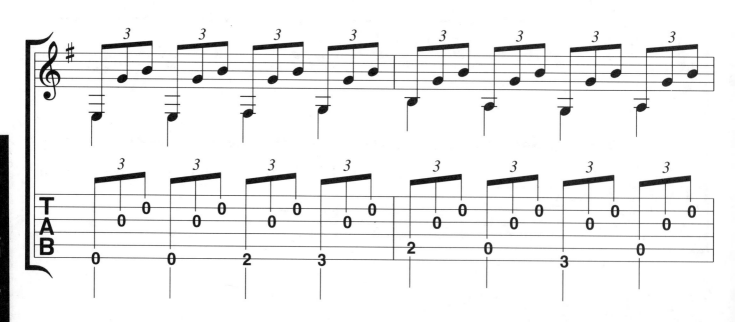

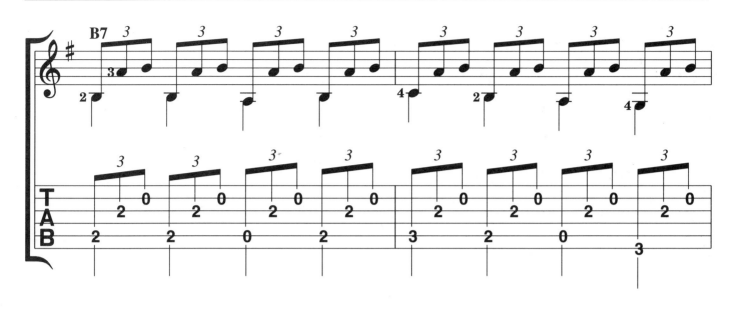

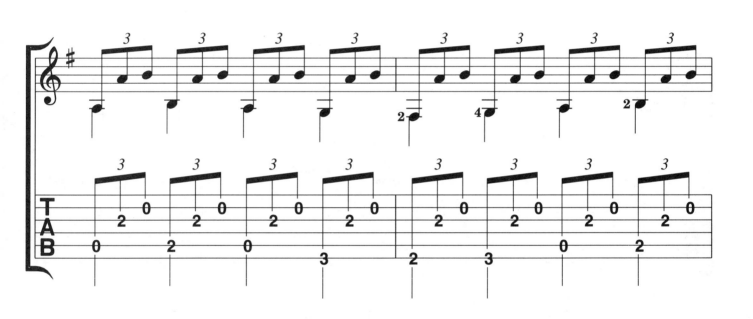

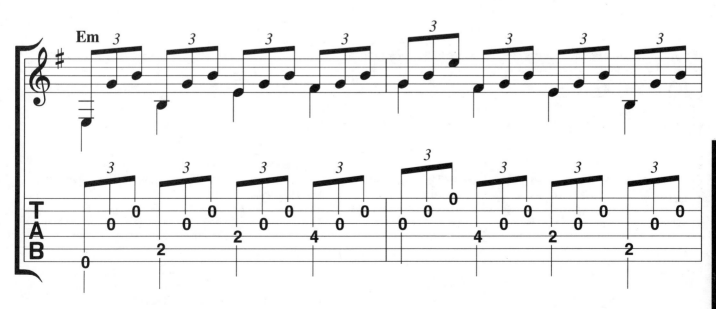

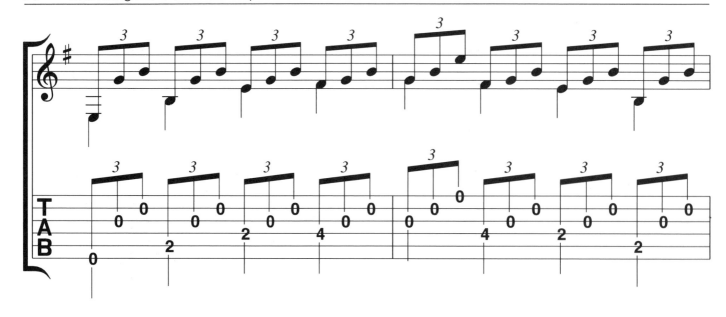

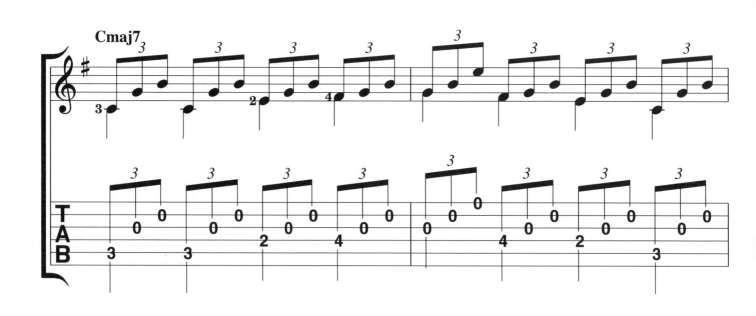

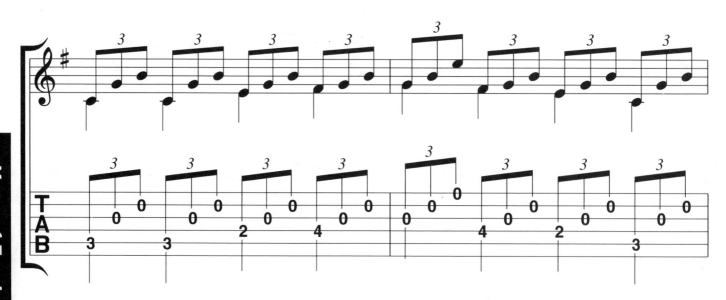

Key of E minor

Andantino

Dionisio Aguado

Key of D

Key of D

Picking Studies

WB

WB

WB

WB

Key of D

⑤

WB

⑥

WB

⑦

WB

⑧

WB

Key of D

(9)   WB

(10)   WB

(11)   WB

(12) **Dropped-D Tuning**   WB

6 = D

Key of D

(13) Dropped-D Tuning   WB

6 = D

(14) Dropped-D Tuning   WB

6 = D

(15)   WB

(16)   WB

Cross Picking Studies

① Dropped-D Tuning   WB
6 = D

② Dropped-D Tuning   WB
6 = D

③ Dropped-D Tuning   WB
6 = D

④ Dropped-D Tuning   WB
6 = D

* In dropped D tuning - This G is played or the 5th fret - 6th String

Chord Studies

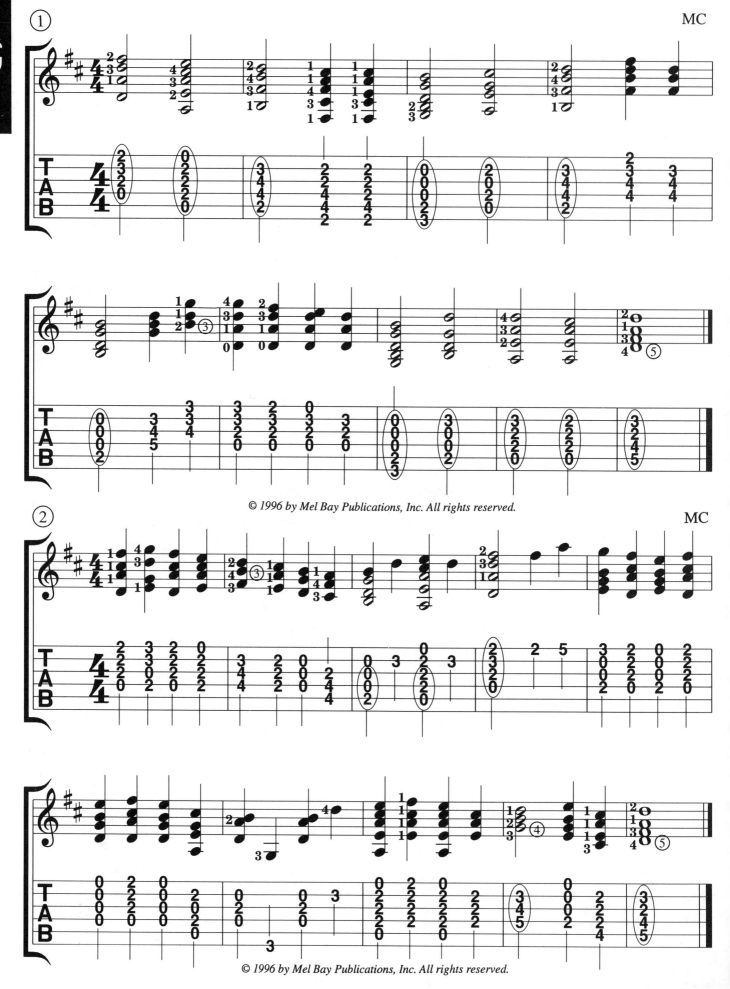

Key of D

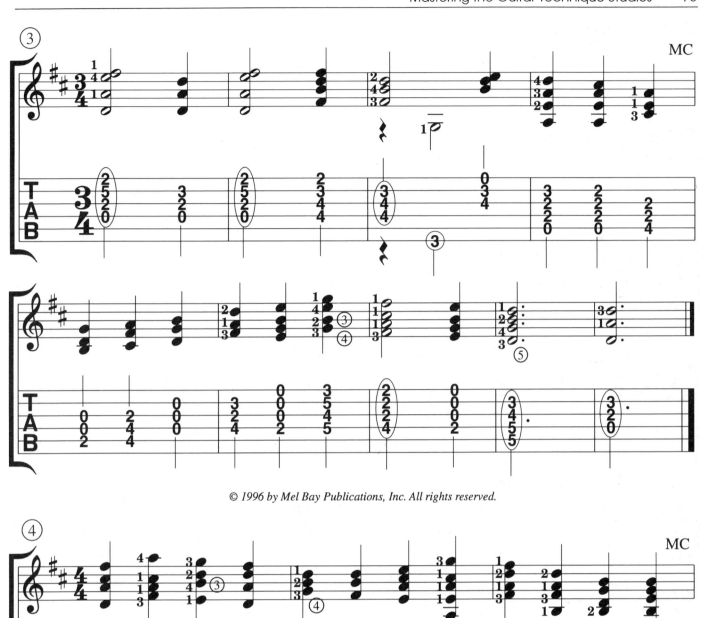

Fingerstyle Studies

Emily's Waltz

Key of D

Recovery

MC

Dropped-D Tuning

Bright ♩ = 118

Key of D

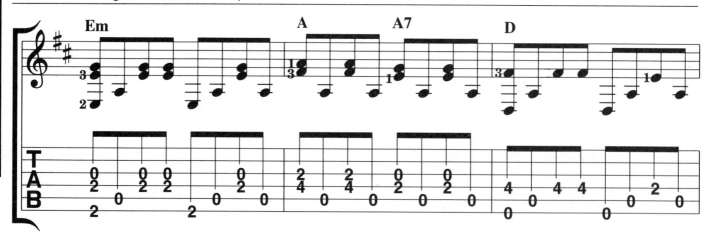

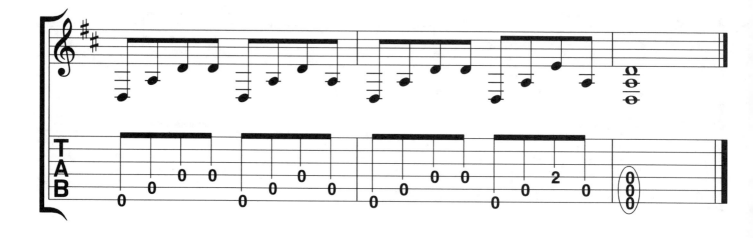

Minuet in D

Robert de Visée

Key of A

Picking Studies

WB

WB

WB

Key of A

Key of A

WB

(8)

WB

(9)

WB

(10)

WB

(11)

WB

WB

Key of A

Finger Agility Studies

WB

Cross Picking Studies

Chord Studies

Key of A

Fingerstyle Studies

Card Tricks

MC

Key of A

Key of A

Song for Kathy

MC

Brightly ♩ = 118

Key of A

Key of A

Waltz

Ferdinando Carulli

Key of A

Key of A

Key of E

Picking Studies

Key of E

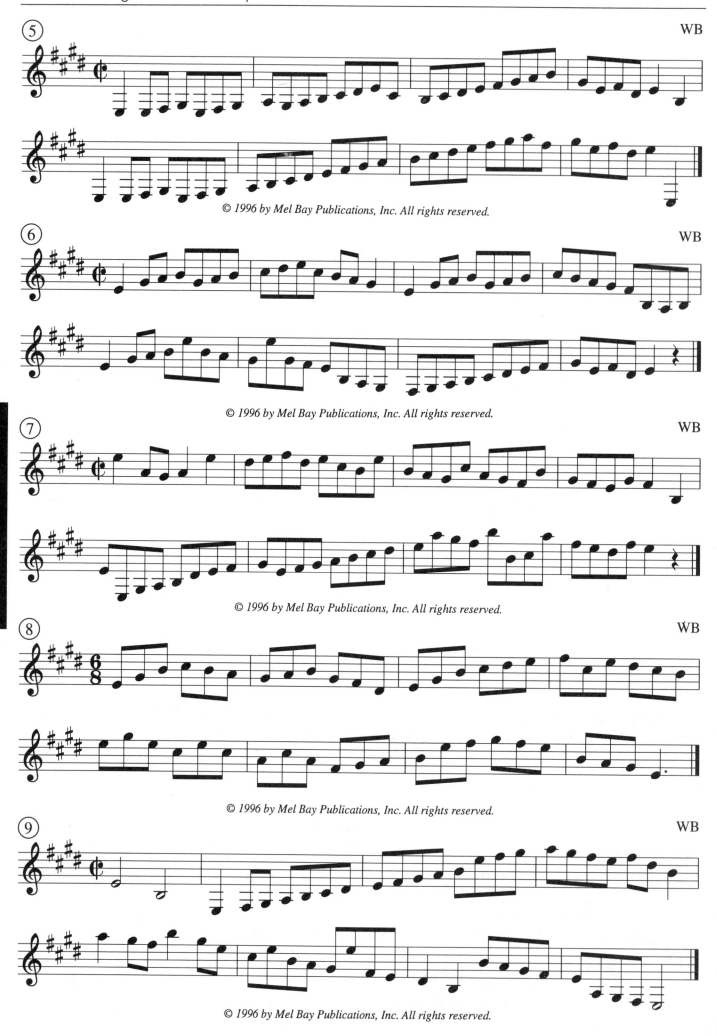

5   WB

6   WB

7   WB

8   WB

9   WB

Key of E

WB

⑩

WB

⑪

WB

⑫

WB

⑬

Key of E

WB

(14)

WB

(15)

WB

(16)

Moveable Finger Patterns

WB

Cross Picking Studies

Key of E

Chord Studies

Key of E

Fingerstyle Studies

Awakening

Key of E

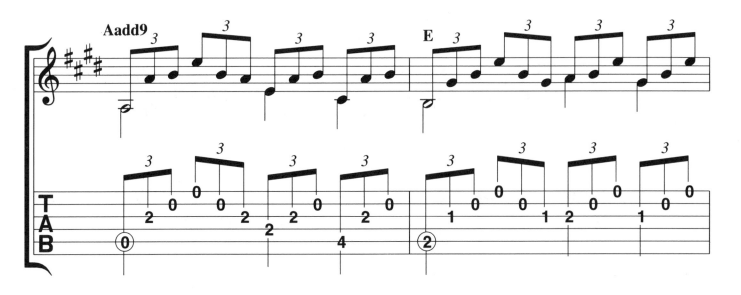

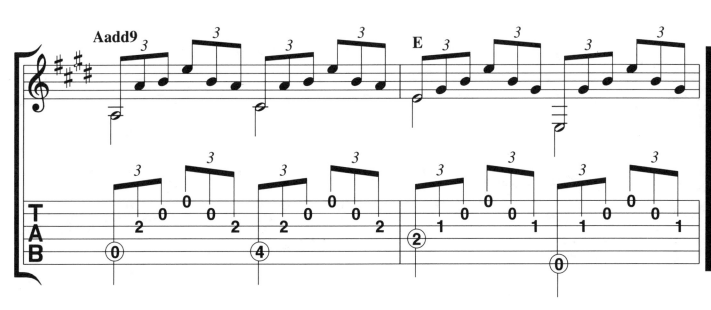

Key of E

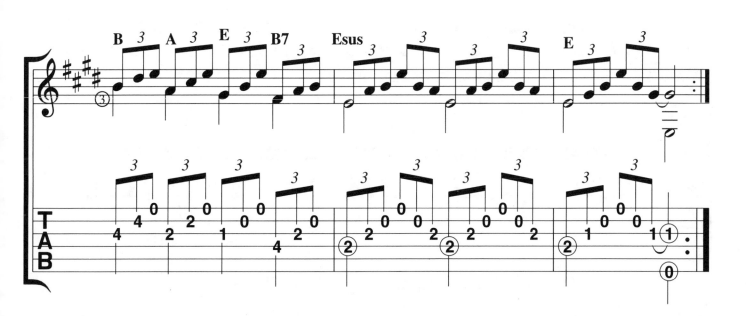

Breaking Away

MC

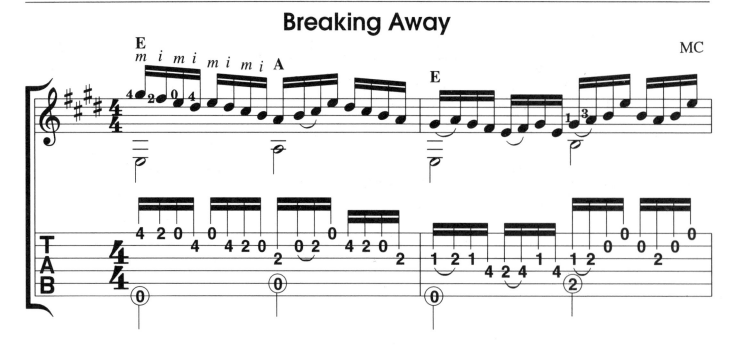

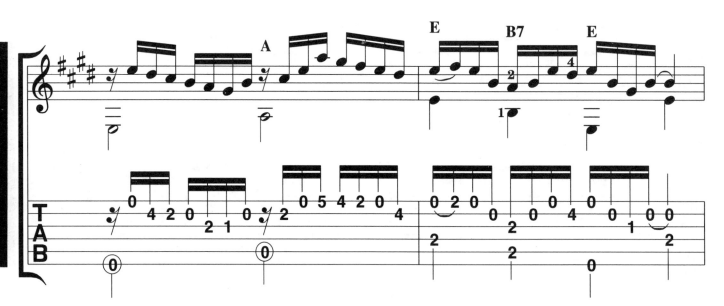

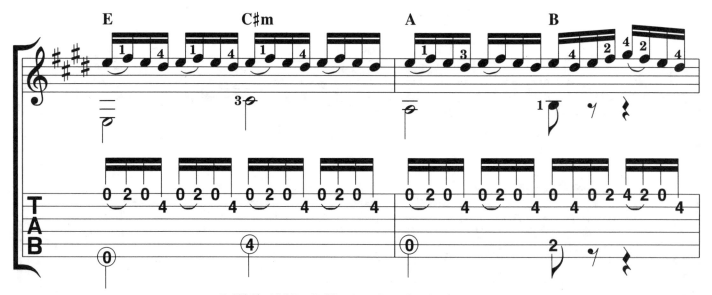

Key of E

Andantino

Mauro Giuliani

Key of E

Key of E

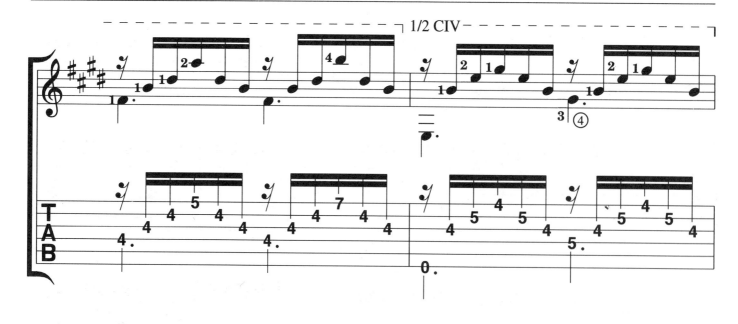

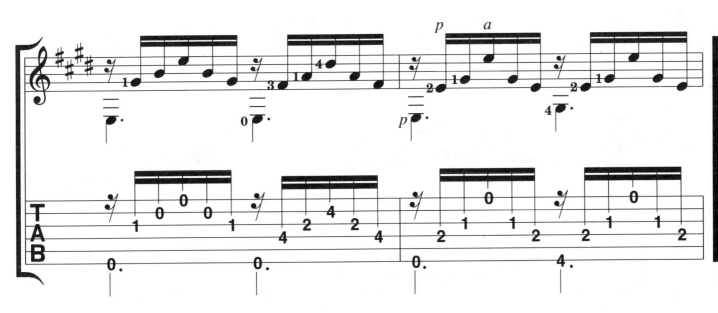

Key of E

Key of F

Picking Studies

Key of F

⑨

WB

⑩

WB

⑪

WB

⑫

WB

Key of F

(13)   WB

(14)   WB

(15)   WB

Finger Agility Pattern

WB

Key of F

Cross Picking Studies

Key of F

Chord Studies

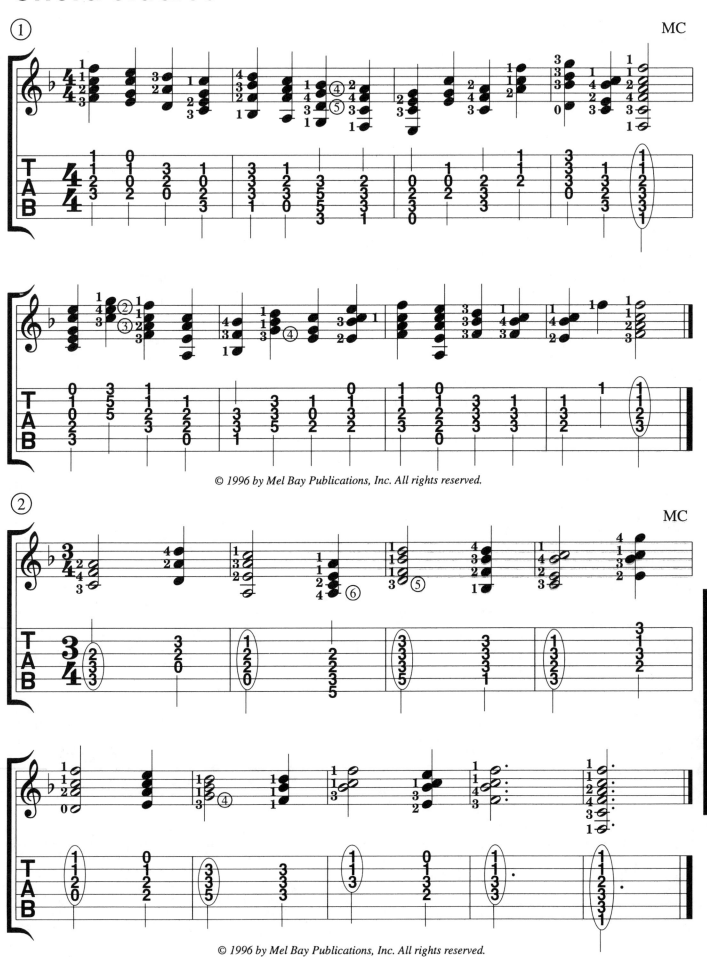

Key of F

Key of F

Fingerstyle Studies

Golden Fields

MC

Key of F

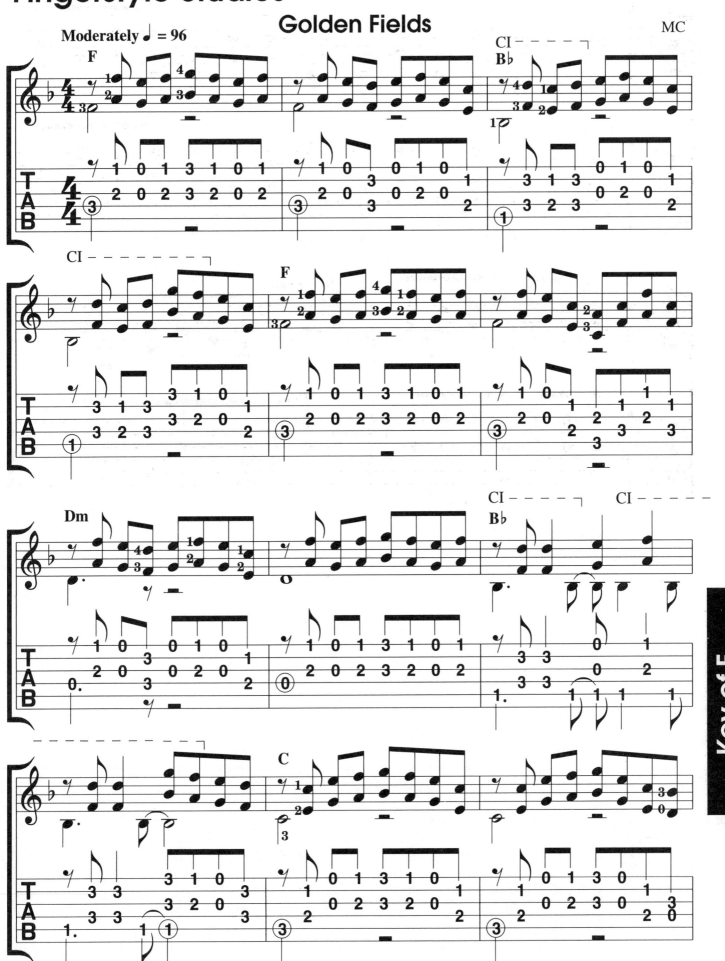

Gentle Kiss

Key of F

Key of F

Andante

Ferdinando Carulli

Key of D minor

Picking Studies

WB

①

WB

②

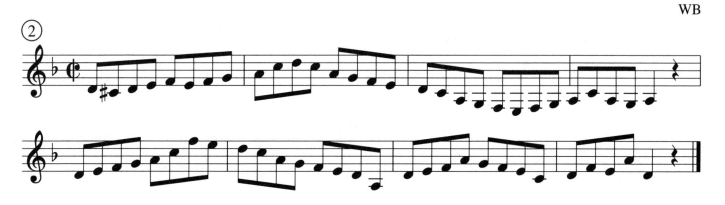

WB

③

WB

④

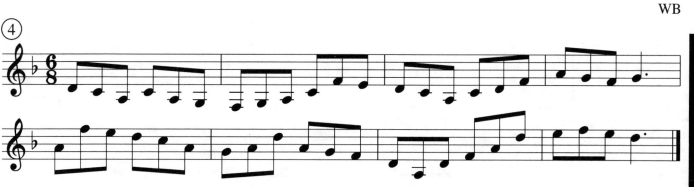

Key of D minor

Dropped-D Tuning

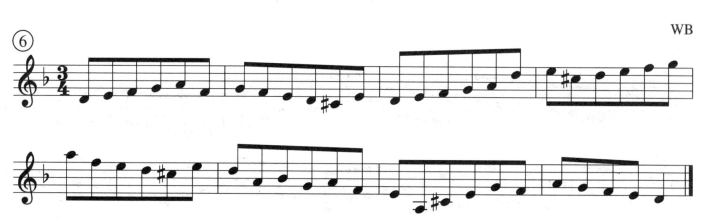

Key of D minor

Dropped-D Tuning

⑨ 6 = D   WB

Dropped-D Tuning

⑩ 6 = D   WB

⑪   WB

⑫   WB

⑬   WB

Key of D minor

(14) Dropped-D Tuning

(15)   WB

Finger Agility Studies

WB

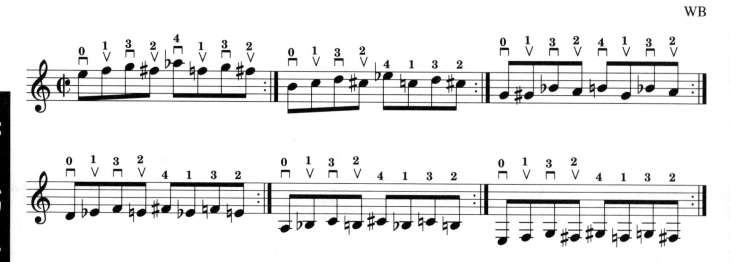

Key of D minor

Cross Picking Studies

Dropped-D Tuning

① 6 = D   WB

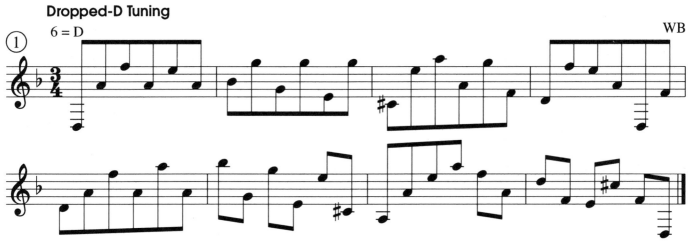

Dropped-D Tuning

② 6 = D   WB

③   WB

Dropped-D Tuning

④ 6 = D   WB

Key of D minor

Chord Studies

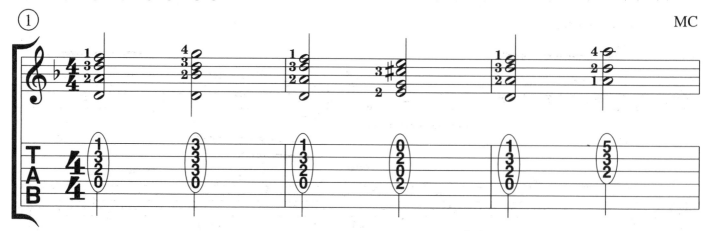

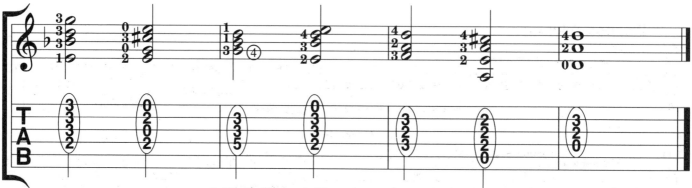

Key of D minor

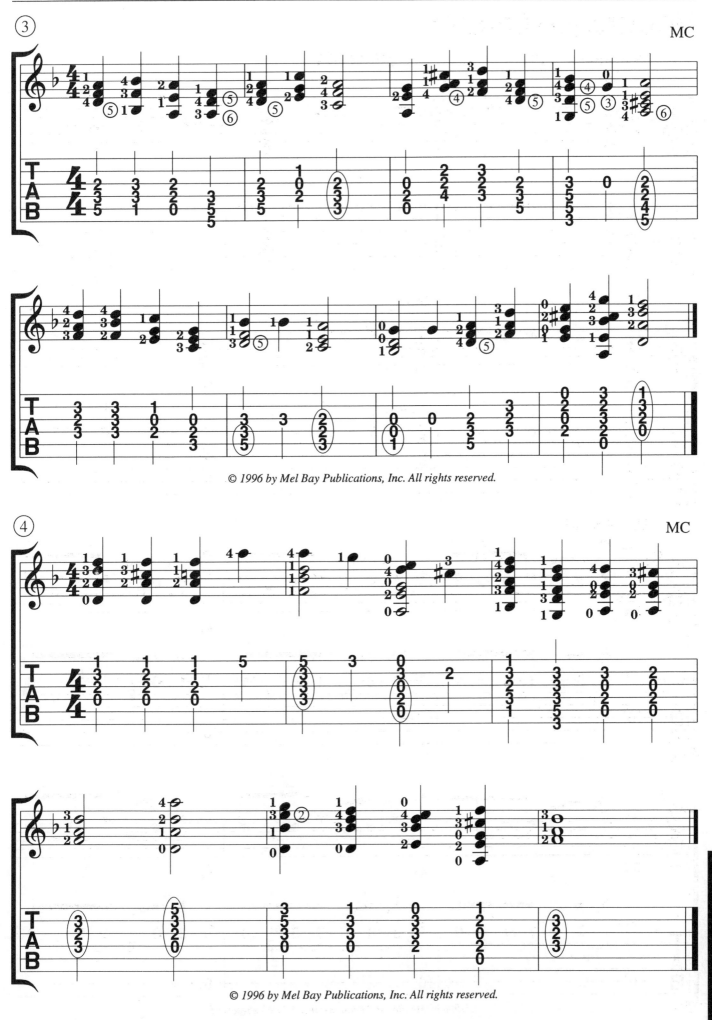

Key of D minor

Fingerstyle Studies

Secrets

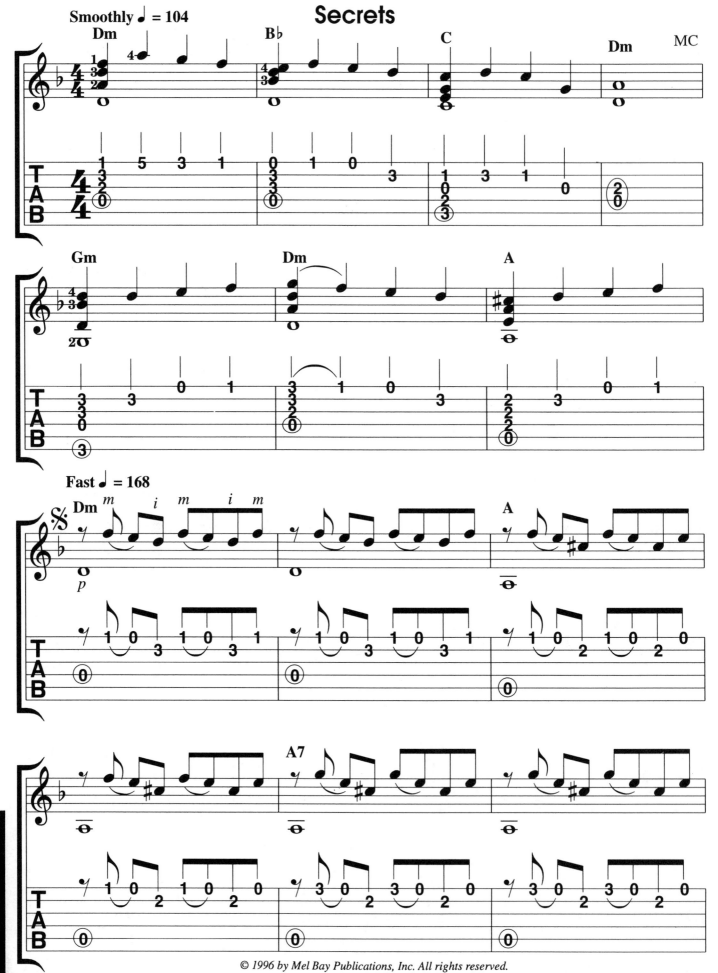

Key of D minor

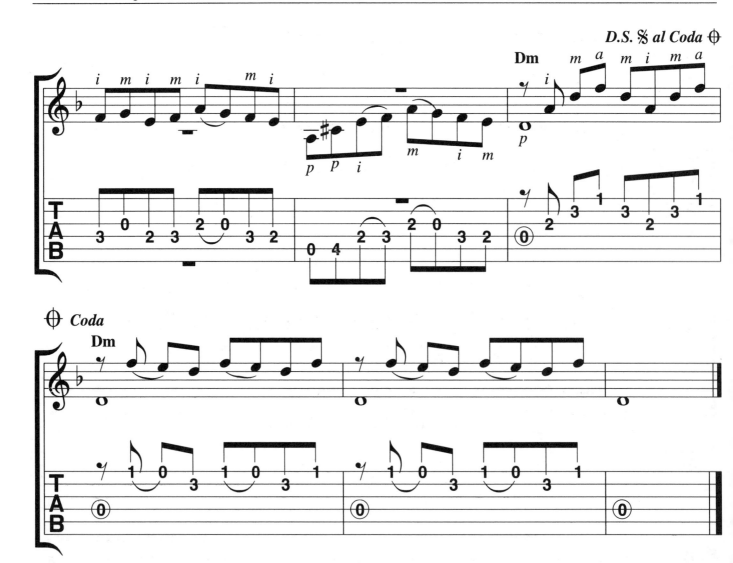

El Castillo

MC

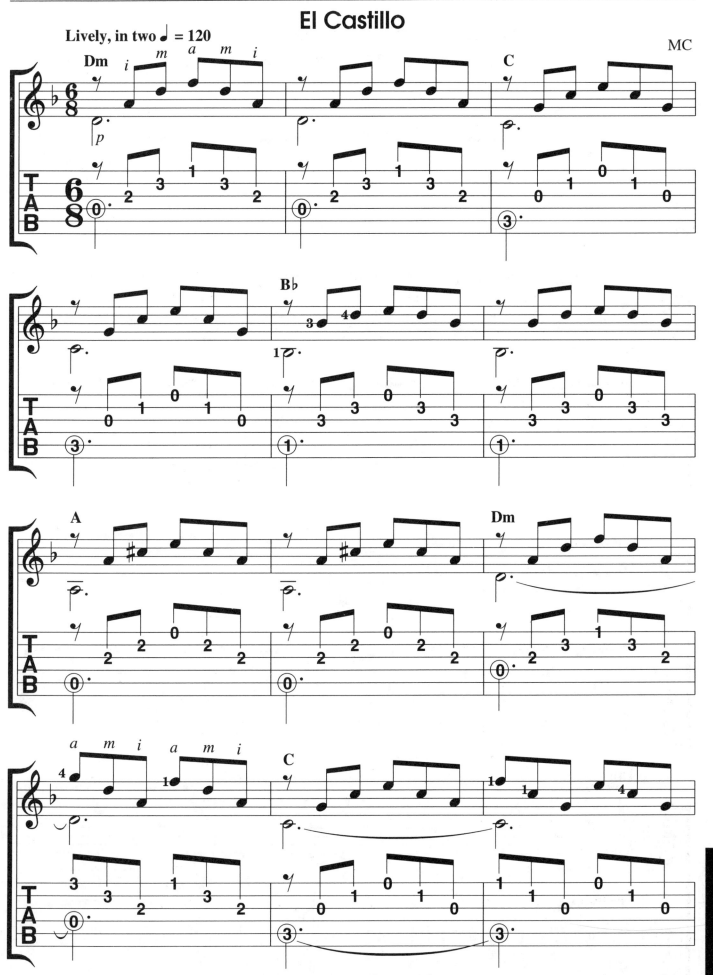

Key of D minor

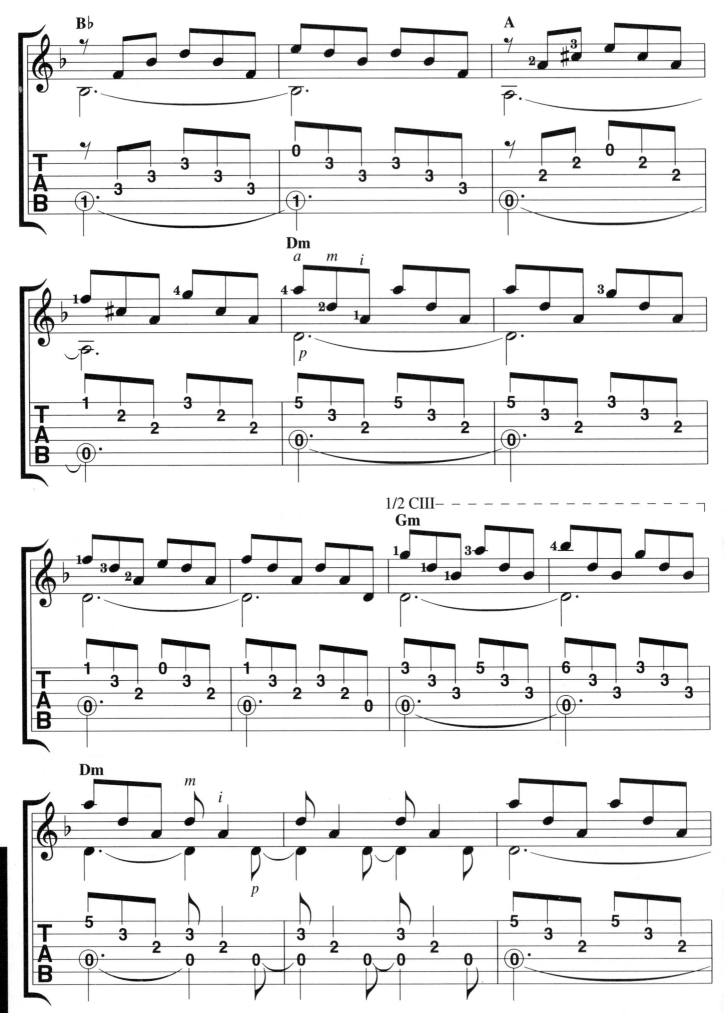

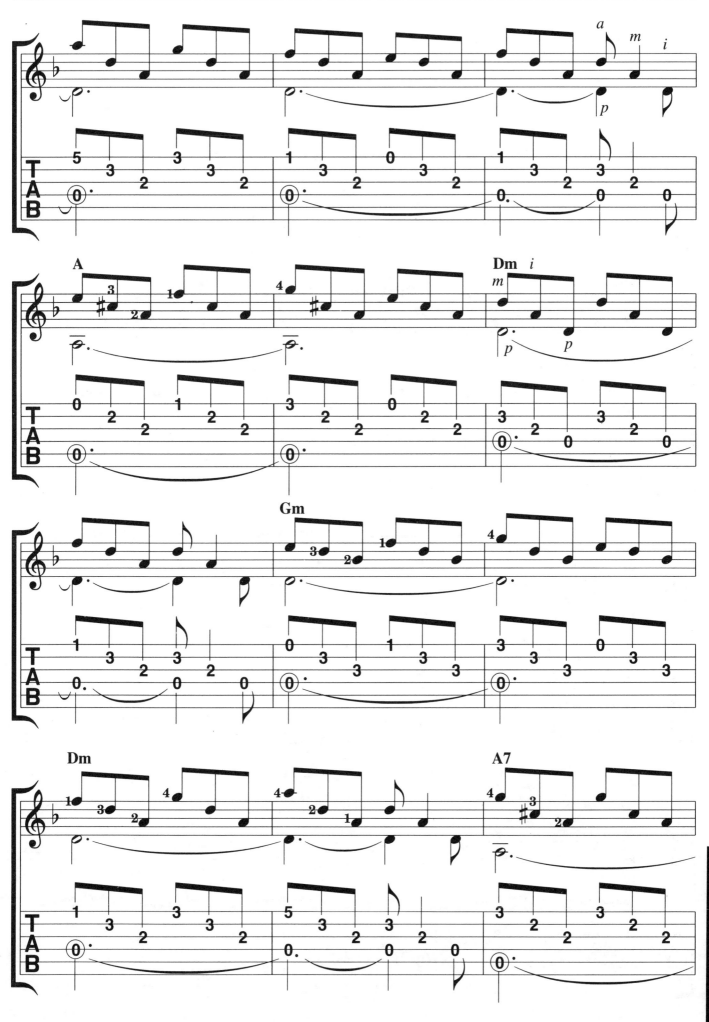

Key of D minor

Bouree

Robert de Visée

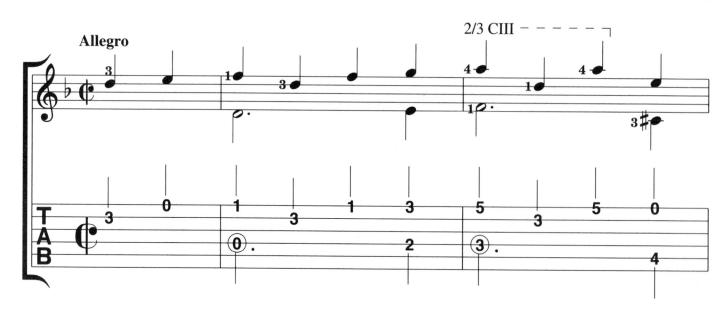

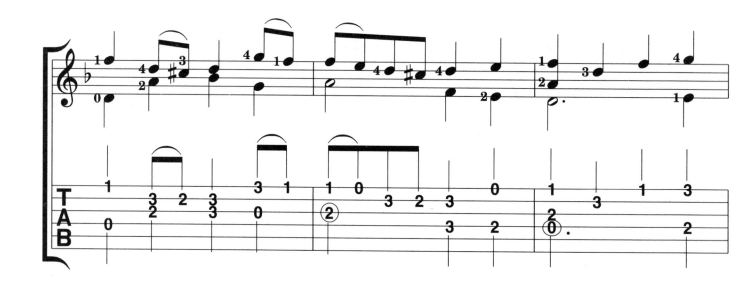

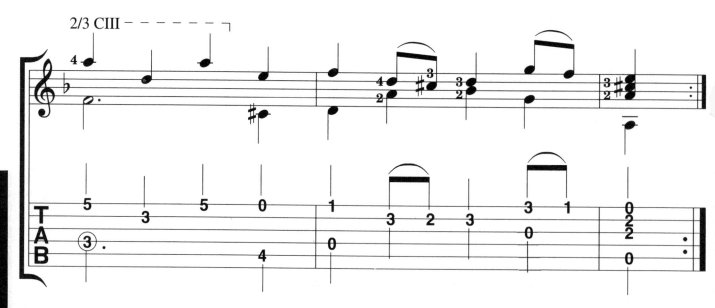

Key of D minor

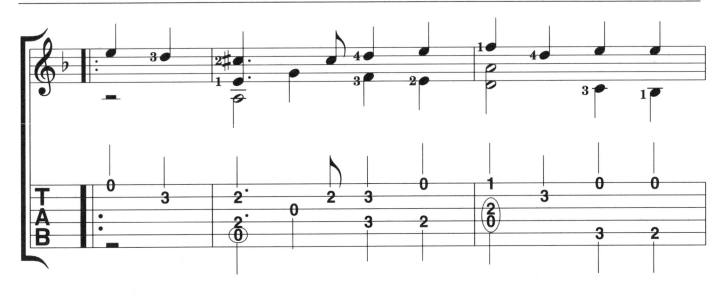

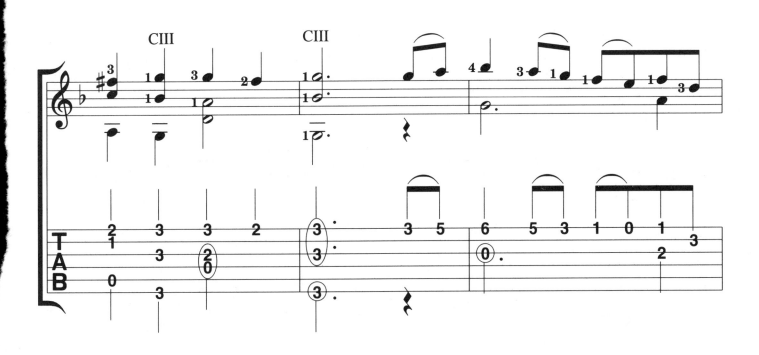

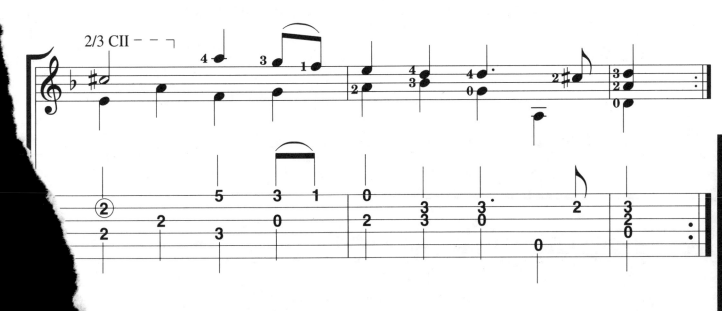

Key of D minor

Key of B♭

Key of B♭

Picking Studies

WB

WB

WB

WB

Key of B♭

WB

⑤

WB

⑥

WB

⑦

WB

⑧

Key of B♭

WB

⑨

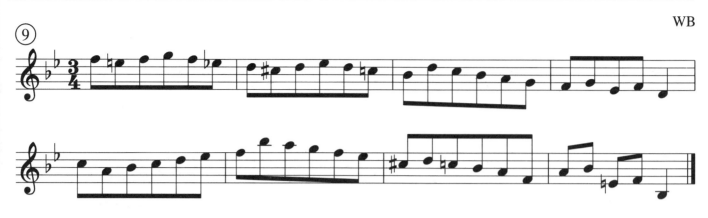

WB

⑩

WB

⑪

WB

⑫

Key of B♭

(13)   WB

(14)   WB

(15)   WB

Finger Agility Pattern

WB

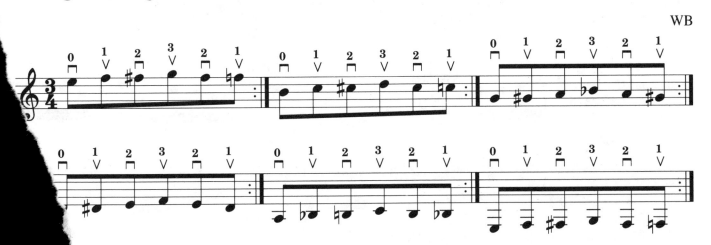

Cross Picking Studies

Chord Studies

① MC

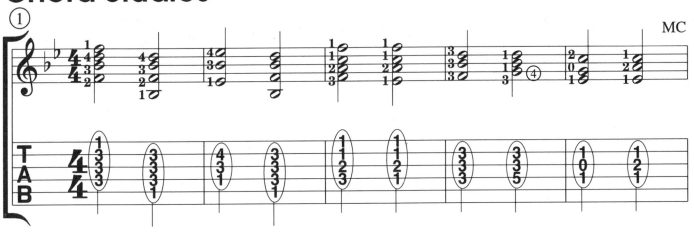

② MC

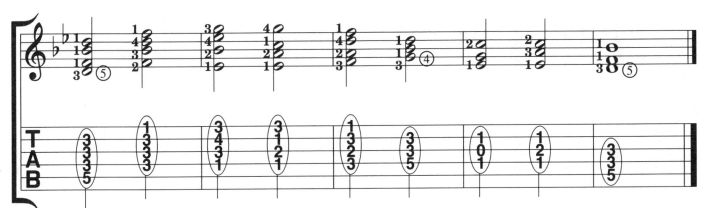

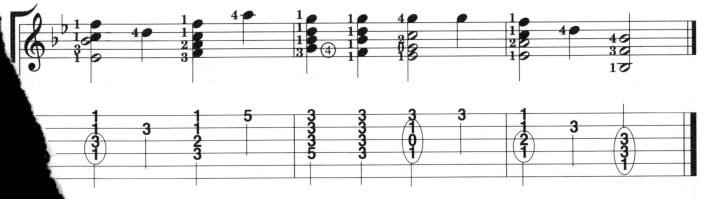

Key of B♭

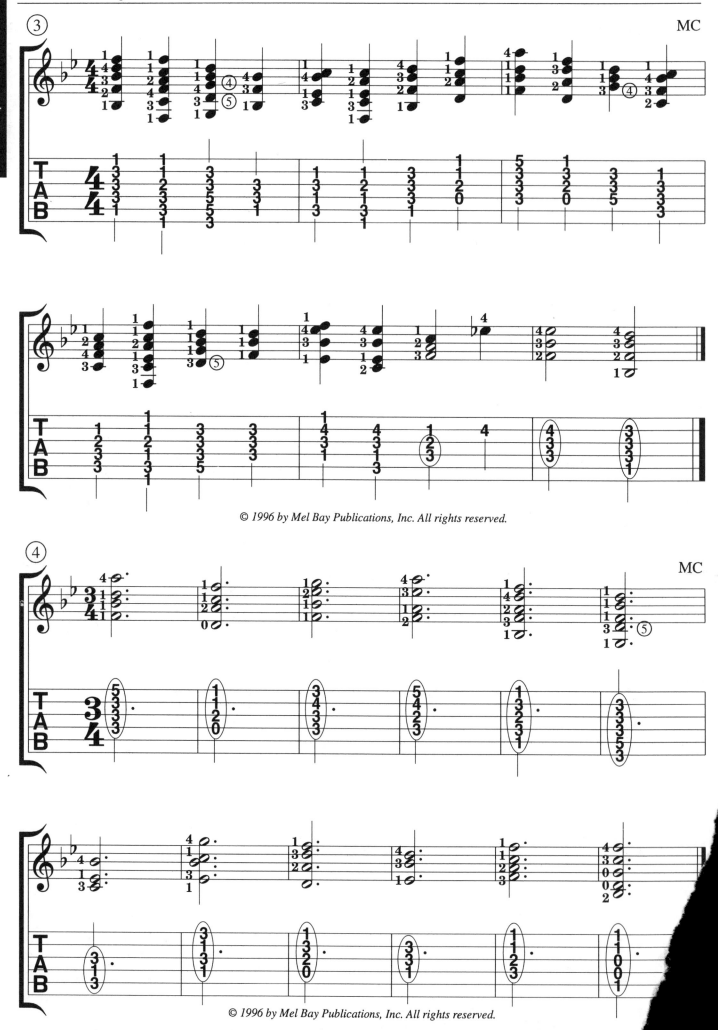

Fingerstyle Studies

Long Time

Brightly ♩ = 144

(In each measure, hold the chords as much as possible)

MC

Key of B♭

Mirage

Moderately, let notes ring ♩ = 104

MC

Key of B♭

Key of B♭

Prelude in B♭

Francesco Molino

Key of B♭

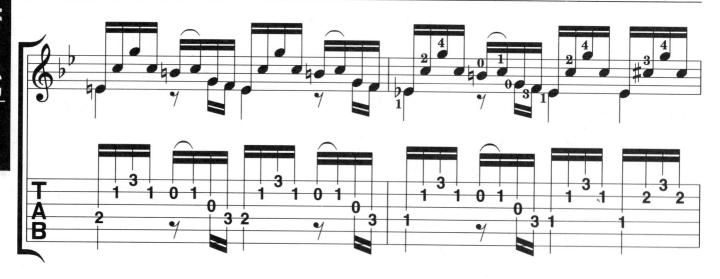

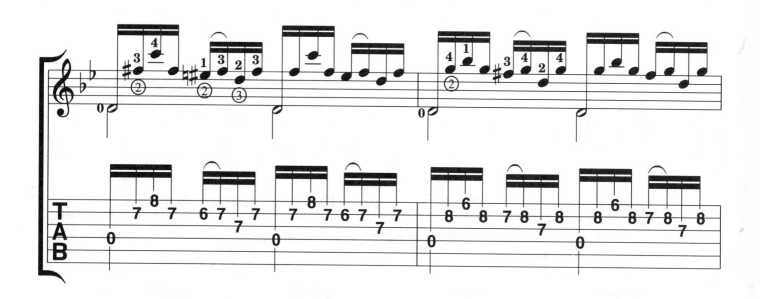

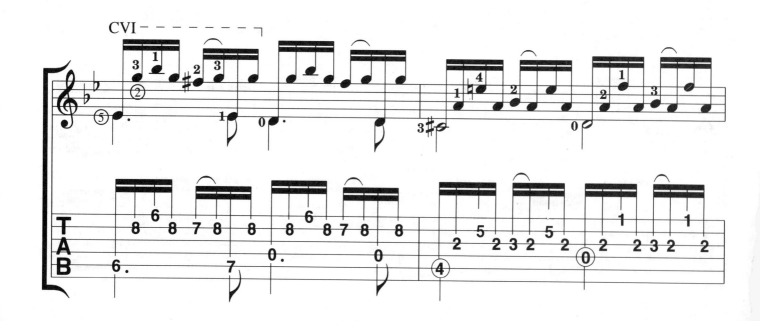

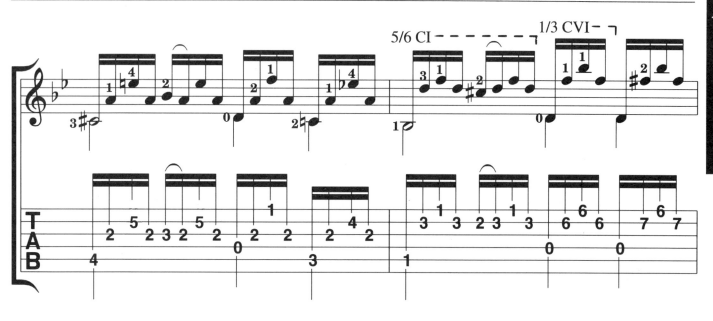

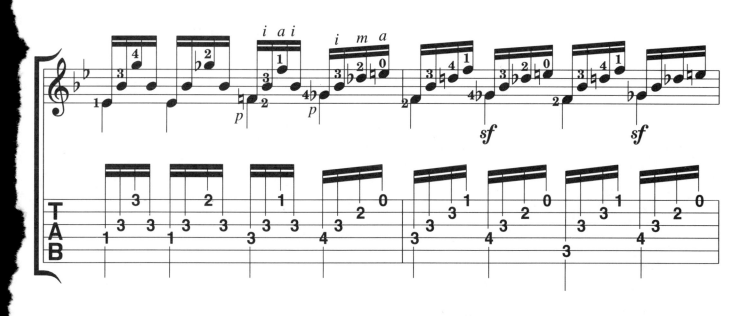

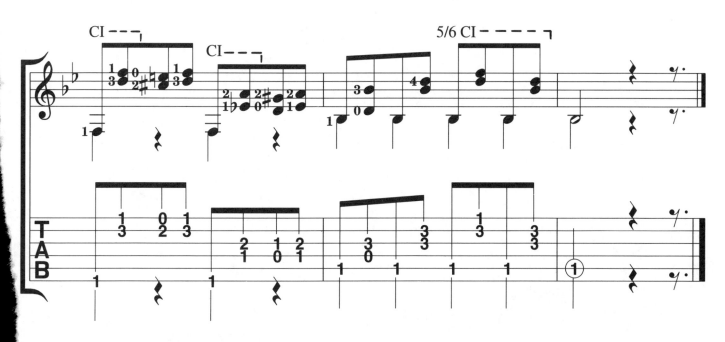